PRODUCER COMPENSATION

Young Agents Committee
Independent Insurance Agents of Georgia

The National Underwriter Company
420 East Fourth Street
Cincinnati, Ohio 45202

Copyright © 1981 by
THE NATIONAL UNDERWRITER COMPANY
420 East Fourth Street
Cincinnati, Ohio 45202

All rights reserved

First Edition, Second Printing

Library of Congress Catalog Number 81-83643
International Standard Book Number 0-87218-314-9

PRODUCER COMPENSATION COMMITTEE

A. Byron Downs, Jr., CPCU — Co-Chairman
The Rohrabaugh Co.
Atlanta, Georgia

Harold R. Turner, CPCU — Co-Chairman
Partner
Merritt and McKenzie
Atlanta, Georgia

Dwight Bagwell, President
Bagwell-Padgett Insurance
Augusta, Georgia

Andrew M. Beck III
Commercial Underwriting Manager
Reese Huffman Company
Rome, Georgia

Ronald F. Hale, CPCU
Account Executive
The Jordan Agency, Inc.
Columbus, Georgia

Geary C. Langford, CLU — President
Caldwell and Langford
Thomasville, Georgia

Dennis O. Lofton
Jones and Hill Insurance
Savannah, Georgia

Charles E. Malmquist, Vice President
Potter — Holden and Company
Atlanta, Georgia

Sheila Maynard
First American Insurance Agency, Inc.
Atlanta, Georgia

CONTRIBUTORS

G. Woody Cole
Carroll Realty and Insurance Co.
Carrollton, Georgia

Erwin James Eldridge III
Athens Insurers, Inc.
Athens, Georgia

John W. Honaker
Tri-County Insurance Agency
Carrollton, Georgia

Robert H. McEver
McEver and Company
Atlanta, Georgia

J. Robert Sutter
Pritchard and Jerden, Inc.
Atlanta, Georgia

PREFACE

All independent agencies must confront the problems of producer compensation and agency perpetuation, while also striving to build solid agency growth. The heart of the agency is the producer. He or she is the person responsible for soliciting and obtaining clients and then reselling these clients each year. The key to an agency's success is largely dependent on the relationship that exists between the producers and the principal.

The agency should strive to obtain the very best producers available. To obtain and, more importantly, to retain these individuals, the agency must develop a career path that will clearly outline how the individual will be compensated and what he or she can expect to receive if he or she reaches the performance goals. One of the unique aspects of the property and casualty insurance career is that it provides not only an opportunity to earn a substantial income, but also the opportunity to participate in the earnings of the firm.

There are many ways to arrange a compensation program for a producer of a property and casualty agency; the authors of this publication have no intention of offering a

Preface

panacea. What we would like to do, however, is provide insights into the components of compensation programs, as well as suggest some plans that can be used effectively.

The ideal compensation plan is one which is equally beneficial to the producer and to the agency. We have tried to establish time-frames for producer compensation plans because, as producers mature, their needs and lifestyles may change and the program that they began with may well be inadequate to serve individual requirements in later stages of their career.

This book was written by the producer compensation subcommittee of Young Agents of Georgia. This is a committee of the Independent Insurance Agents of Georgia. We would like to thank not only the young agents and agency principals who contributed valuable input to the authors, but also employers of the authors for donating time and effort to make this publication possible. In addition, we would like to thank the Rough Notes Company, Inc., 1200 North Meridian Street, Indianapolis, Indiana for permission to use the results of "What it Costs to Run An Insurance Agency — 1979 Edition." This material was adapted for use in Chapter 8.

Our grateful appreciation also goes to W. Dan McDonald, CPCU, and J. Clifford McCurry, CPCU, who conceptualized this publication and supported us through its completion. It is impossible to list all of the persons who contributed to this project, but we also would like to recognize Fred W. McGinty, CPCU, Chairman of the Young Agents Committee for his diligence and encouragement.

Harold R. Turner, CPCU
A. Byron Downs, Jr., CPCU
Atlanta, Georgia

CONTENTS

Producer Compensation Committee iii
Contributors v
Preface vii
Contents ix
List of Figures xi
List of Tables xiii

1 The Fundamental Agent/Producer Relationship 1
    Introduction
    Planning for the New Producer
    Reasons for Entering the Agency Business
    Prospecting for the New Producer
    Making the Proper Selection

2 Job Description and Goal Setting 7
    Responsibility and Authority
    Short Term Goals
    Intermediate Goals
    Long Term Goals

3 Traditional Elements of Producer Compensation 15
    Group Insurance
    Life Insurance
    Automobile Expense
    Expense Accounts

Contents

    Vacations
    Education — Association Expense
    Retirement Plans
    Employee Stock Option Plans
    Intangibles

4 Relationship of Motivation to Producer Compensation 25

    Motivational Factors
    Survey Results

5 Agency Ownership 35

    Ownership as Motivation
    Transferring Ownership

6 Developing A Producer Compensation Plan 43

    Short Range Goals
    Intermediate Range Goals
    Long Range Goals
    Conclusion

7 Auxiliary Staff Functions 61

    Benefits
    Responsibilities
    Methods of Remuneration

8 The Time Line of an Insurance Agency 71

Appendix 81

Index 103

LIST OF FIGURES

Figure		Page
1	Need Hierachy	30
2	Compensation or Fringe Benefits Indicated As "Very Important"	33
3	Sink-Or-Swim Plan	44
4	All-Encompassing Plan	45
5	Commission Only Plan	50
6	Commission/Draw Plan	51
7	Salary Only Plan	51
8	Combination Commission and Salary Plan	52
9	Validation Schedule	53
10	Intermediate Stage Compensation Plan	56
11	Long Range Compensation Plan	58
12	Agency Premium	78
13	Total Compensation to Owners	79
14	Owners' Equity	80

LIST OF TABLES

Table *Page*

1 The ABC Insurance Agency Income Statement (1981).. 72

2 The ABC Insurance Agency Income Statement (1983).. 73

3 The ABC Insurance Agency Income Statement (1985).. 74

4 The ABC Insurance Agency Income Statement (1990).. 75

5 The ABC Insurance Agency Income Statement (1995).. 76

6 The ABC Insurance Agency Income Statement (2000).. 77

CHAPTER 1

The Fundamental Agent/Producer Relationship

Introduction

The key to successful agency/producer relationship requires a clear understanding of each party's expectations of the other. Such an understanding cannot be achieved without the agency first having an organized plan and method of hiring and developing the new producer's talents.

The purpose of this chapter is to discuss the initial planning and prospecting requisites of the new producer, including the hiring and goal setting attributes.

Planning for the New Producer

The agency must analyze its individual needs, both current and long-term, in order to establish what capacity the new producer will serve. The function of the new producer

Producer Compensation

can vary considerably according to the agency's geographic location, type of business it produces, and its volume. For example, a new producer of an agency located in smaller towns and cities would more than likely be involved in handling all lines of insurance, whereas, the new producer in larger metropolitan areas would probably be required to handle a specialized class of business.

In any event, the agency must identify what area of the business requires assistance, and must determine the resources available to compensate the new producer.

The function of the new producer can be directed toward any of the following:
- Personal Lines
- Commercial Lines
- Both Personal and Commercial Lines
- Sales Person Only
- Inside Person or Placer of Business

Reasons for Entering the Agency Business

While it is important for the agency to make plans prior to actually prospecting for a new producer, it is equally important for the agency to recognize the motivating factors that will encourage an individual to enter the agency business. Such a recognition is important for the hiring agency in order to enable it to work within these motivating factors when hiring and developing the new producer.

The income derived from agency business for a producer can be a motivating factor because of its flexibility. It is possible for the producer to be compensated in direct proportion to his or her performance. The producer-agency business relationship also is somewhat unique in that the producer may negotiate his or her compensation.

One of the more controversial issues of the relationship is ownership. Because an agency, generally speaking, is a small business, the ability of the agency to offer some form of ownership is an alternative.

The apparent need for improved management in the agency system offers a new producer the early opportunity to move into management. Agencies recognize the benefit of employee education and training, too. For this reason, the producer, in many instances, will have his or her education and training funded by the agency.

After achieving credentials within the industry, the producer should attain career mobility and market ability. And, since the agency system enjoys a reputation of professionalism, the new producer can also be looked upon with respect as a professional. The effect of all of these motivating factors provides considerable potential to the new producer, depending on his or her aspirations.

Prospecting for the New Producer

Where an agency can find a new producer is a common question for which there are several answers. If an agency desires to hire someone without business experience, recruiting from the college ranks is one choice. This alternative is especially desirable to the agency that prefers to perform the actual grass roots training. And it is likely to entail less expense, from the standpoint of initial salary expense, at least, than if an otherwise experienced person were to be hired. One of the possible drawbacks of recruiting a college graduate is that it may be difficult to determine whether such person is sincere in pursuing an agency career and is mature enough to handle the serious responsibilities of the job.

If an agency prefers an individual with some prior business experience, some good prospects may be available from within the banking, finance and sales industries. Individuals

Producer Compensation

within these industries offer distinct advantages, because of their business contacts, their expertise and/or knowledge of business function in general, and, perhaps, their maturity. All of these attributes of an individual, particularly business contacts, could open the door to an agency's production. If such individual possesses strong sales ability, that could be a plus, since, when combined with the agency's training, it could result in a profitable combination to the individual as well as to the agency.

One potential problem of prospecting from within a non-insurance industry is that the individual may have financial obligations and/or demands which may be difficult for the agency to meet. This potential problem is no different from that encountered by other businesses, however. If the job shows promise to both the individual and the business, perhaps the major obstacles for having a meeting of the minds can be worked out by compromise.

If an agency desires someone with insurance experience, prospects may be available from other agencies or from insurance companies. Those who already have some experience in insurance will obviously provide advantages, because it is likely that the agency's time and cost in training will be minimized. Of course, it may cost the agency more in hiring some experienced person, but the rate of return on such investment may be better than if an unskilled person were to be hired instead.

Hiring a person who is experienced in insurance may still present some problems. For example, a person hired from another agency may have difficulty adapting to another agency's operation, including its personnel. The same type of problem could arise when a person is hired from the insurance company ranks. Yet, problems of this nature are no different from those confronting other businesses. It is, to some extent, a chance that has to be taken. The opportunity for long-term financial growth, including the option for ownership may help to overcome some of these problems. What also may help to alleviate problems, are the necessary steps that should be taken when making the proper selection of an applicant.

Making the Proper Selection

The agency that desires to make the proper selection of an applicant must review thoroughly the applicant's resume, because it will reveal the talents, experience, and perhaps, the job stability of such person. The personal interview should also be conducted in an atmosphere that is conducive to a free flow of information between the applicant and the interviewer.

The agency's objective in the interview should be to inform the applicant of his or her role and objectives, and to also determine whether the applicant is receptive to the responsibilities of the job. (This subject is discussed more fully in Chapter 2.) If the applicant is inexperienced, formal testing can be a useful tool in divulging the applicant's potential.

If the applicant appears to meet the agency's criteria, it also may be helpful for the agency principal to conduct an informal session with the applicant's spouse in order to learn more about the applicant and his or her spouse's attitude of the new job.

CHAPTER 2

Job Description and Goal Setting

Once the selection process of prospecting is completed, it is important that the new producer get off on the right foot. A proper beginning is founded on a clear understanding between the agency and the producer as to the new producer's responsibilities and goals. The most effective means of establishing this understanding is through the formulation of a written job description that includes goal setting. These two functions, goal setting and the construction of the job description, will often overlap. This is because a job description is nothing more than a plan that outlines responsibilities, specific duties and authority which are necessary to achieve one's goals. Therefore, as a hiring agency approaches the task of constructing a suitable job description for the new producer, it is important to be ever mindful of the goals of the agency, as well as of the producer. The agency should also realize that a job description should be reviewed and updated at regular intervals in order to properly reflect short range, intermediate range and long range goals.

Job descriptions can vary greatly and are dictated by the different needs and goals of the hiring agency. For example, an agency that desires to generate additional revenues would dictate a job description much different from an agency more concerned about agency perpetuation.

A job description should begin with a general statement about the responsibilities of the new producer and then zero in on the specific duties and authorities being granted by the agency. The responsibilities of the new producer should coincide closely with the goals of the hiring agency. Responsibilities not only should be thought of in terms of short range, but also intermediate and long range. Such analysis of goals can be done on a similar basis: Zero to three years, short range; three to ten years, intermediate range; and ten years and over, long range. This close association between responsibilities and goals can be better seen as the responsibilities are reviewed in more detail, followed by a discussion of goals in general.

Responsibility and Authority

Initial responsibilities of the new producer can be categorized as educational and production. As previously noted, responsibilities consist of general statements made at the beginning of the job description. A clear statement concerning educational responsibilities, therefore, should be made to include a definition of these responsibilities, as the acquisition of product knowledge, selling skills and an understanding of agency operations. The statement made with respect to production responsibilities should address itself to both responsibilities, to new accounts, as well as respon-

Job Description—Goal Setting

sibilities to existing accounts. In analyzing intermediate and long range responsibilities, we might see a broadening of responsibilities to include management and, at some later point, ownership and agency perpetuation. Similar statements could be incorporated within the job description to encompass these intermediate and long range responsibilities; however, for the new producer's initial job description it might be well to address only the initial responsibilities.

Having set forth the new producer's responsibilities in a general way, it is necessary now to incorporate within the job description a listing of specific duties to be performed and expected of the new producer. The degree of detail is left up to the discretion of the hiring agency. But it should include, within the listing, his or her duties with regard to prospecting, soliciting, servicing, relationships with others, and finally meeting the goals and objectives as mutually agreed upon. It is certainly not the intent of the listing to have the agency compile all duties of the new producer, but, instead, to use this opportunity to provide the new producer with a checklist of the more important duties.

The final component of the job description is probably the most important. It is in this section that the agency spells out the authority of the new producer. Because of its importance, the statement of authority should be made clear and understandable. Authority should be expressed in terms of binding coverage, quoting and placing business, and assuming and being accountable for all responsibilities given.

For one reason or another, written job descriptions are not utilized by all agencies. But if a written job description can produce a better understanding between the new producer and agency, the chances of a good relationship would certainly improve.

Producer Compensation

Although agency goals and new producer responsibilities coincide in the formation of a job description, such description cannot act as a substitute for goal setting and the establishing of written goals for the new producer. Wherein construction of job description emphasis is placed on the agency's goals, under goal setting an opportunity is given the new producer to express himself or herself and offer input into setting his or her own goals. Written goals are essential to the new producer and the agency as a means of monitoring and measuring the new producer's progress. The agency should offer assistance and also serve as a guide for the new producer in formulating his or her goals. This should be done so that the established goals of the new producer are both realistic and challenging. This joint process of establishing goals will also ensure against improper goal setting where goals may be set that are too difficult or too easy to achieve. Although it is necessary for the agency to provide proper guidance, it is equally necessary for the new producer to feel he or she plays a part in formulation of his or her own goals. As mentioned earlier, goals can be handled on the basis of three broad categories: short range goals, zero to three years; intermediate range goals, three to ten years; and long range goals, ten years to retirement. Both the new producer and the agency should establish their goals with respect to all three categories.

Short Term Goals

Short range goals of the agency center around the proper training and direction of the new producer; whereas, the new producer's short range goals are overshadowed by desire to maintain a reasonable income. The reasons for training the new producer are simple. Without proper instruction, the new producer stands little chance of ever

Job Description—Goal Setting

being productive for the agency or himself or herself. Methods of training the new producer are many and varied. For this reason, an educational plan or schedule should be devised to coordinate the training efforts of the agency. The agency's obligation to the new producer is to offer him or her continued instruction. This instruction should provide the producer with product knowledge, selling techniques, and a clear understanding of the agency's overall operations. Because of the average size of most agencies, there exists inadequate staff and time to train new producers. Where this problem exists the agency's role in training the producer can be augmented by the many company schools and association training programs available.

Reasonable income for the new producer may be defined as an amount sufficient to meet his or her needs. These needs may be real, as well as imagined. Real needs consist of the basic needs of food, shelter and clothing or in short, an income sufficient to support his or her family. Imagined needs, on the other hand, are not so readily identified and are much more complex. Imagined needs encompass the image the individual has of himself or herself in order to be successful. An example might be the new producer who feels that country club membership, expensive clothes and exotic cars are necessary for his or her proper image. Although imagined needs are the most difficult to fully understand, they should by no means be ignored when determining a reasonable income.

As the new producer obtains knowledge and confidence in his or her own abilities, it can be expected that his or her sales will increase, allowing the agency to realize both increased growth and volume, as well as increased profits.

Producer Compensation

Intermediate Goals

Turning toward intermediate range goals, one will see the importance of retaining the new producer and outlining his or her continued development through education and motivation. The retention of a new producer is as important as the initial selection process. Everyone loses when a new producer fails. The agency, in hiring the new producer, has varying degrees of investment and training in hiring that person. In order to recoup the initial investment, the agency must retain the producer. The agency can only enjoy the maximum benefit from the new business developed by the new producer through his or her retention. Because he or she was responsible for establishing the relationship with this business he or she is the best suited for servicing and retaining it.

The ability of an agency to retain a new producer is dependent upon the actions of the agency. The agency is expected to provide good working conditions that lend itself to the development and growth of the new producer. Good leadership and guidance for the new producer should be both progressive and consistent. There is a direct relationship between the new producer's progress and the guidance and direction afforded him or her by the agency. Compassion plays its part in retaining the new producer. The insurance industry has its peaks and valleys, and so does the new producer. The agency must show compassion for the new producer during these times by acting as a good listener and understanding his or her discouragement, while at the same time offering proper guidance.

The continued development of a new producer hinges upon continuing proper motivation and training. As the consumer of insurance products continues to be more sophisticated, it is important that the agency encourage its producer

Job Description—Goal Setting

to strive for a high degree of professionalism to meet this demand. A professional status can only be obtained by involvement in educational studies and programs such as CPCU, CLU, and CIC. Furthermore, the agency should encourage a new producer to become involved in insurance industry associations on a local, state or national basis. Involvement in these activities will broaden his or her knowledge as to what other professional agents are doing in their perspective areas. Furthermore, this gives the new producer a professional peer group to measure himself or herself against with respect to his or her efforts toward professionalism, as well as the level of success he or she is trying to achieve.

The producer requires incentives to encourage further development. The opportunity for higher income is an incentive when based on the new producer's performance. Higher income alone, however, cannot motivate the producer. He or she must be allowed the opportunities for increased responsibilities, as well as to participate in the agency's decision-making process and direction.

Long Term Goals

An awareness of both the new producer's and agency's long range goals should exist. This awareness should be made a part of the initial goal setting process. The true long range goals of any new producer lie in the security of his or her future with the agency. The new producer is concerned with the perpetuation of the agency and his or her job security in the event there is any change of ownership. The new producer questions whether he or she will have a voice in the direction and operation of the agency, and too, if he or she will be allowed to share in the ownership at some established date. The desires of new producers for future ownership should be discussed and a clear understanding estab-

Producer Compensation

lished early in their relationship. Many agencies fail to recognize future ownership as a long range objective that will continue to motivate their producers.

Timely and continuous monitoring of the new producer's progress is paramount in the success of the relationship. Early detection of problem areas will enable the agency to respond more quickly to the new producer's needs and return him or her to the right track. The agency should establish criteria for reviewing the new producer's progress. This criteria should be written in the form of a performance review and advance knowledge of these criteria should be given to the new producer so he or she has a clear picture as to how performance will be evaluated.

It is important for one to fully realize the impact of the new producer. For the future and continuation of the independent agency system, agencies must hire, train and properly motivate new producers toward becoming agency owners of the future.

CHAPTER 3

Traditional Elements of Producer Compensation

In examining the traditional elements of producer compensation, one will find that there are as many ways to compensate producers as there are agencies. No one formula works within an agency for compensating producers, and with the different personalities of producers, each person's thoughts of compensation vary.

The first item of importance concerning any producer compensation program is the type of salary arrangement to be offered, since the producer has financial obligations that must be met. And, in order to do a good job in selling and in performing other agency functions, he or she must not be continually worrying about a regular paycheck. Webster's Dictionary defines salary as "regular yearly, monthly or weekly compensation paid for services rendered in business or the professions." Thus, the most important word is "regu-

Producer Compensation

lar." As a producer becomes more experienced and is able to build up his or her commissions, the need for regular salary disappears. The producer also becomes more confident in his or her abilities to produce business and, hence, is able to rely on the book of business when the going gets rough.

In order for a producer to be able to drastically increase his or her income, it is necessary that he or she either have a combination salary-bonus arrangement, or a pure commission arrangement. After the producer is able to support himself or herself comfortably and return a profit to the agency on the book of business, the producer will likely feel that he or she should be compensated in a manner that would allow him or her to participate in a greater share of the commission produced.

A bonus arrangement enables the producer to continue to receive his or her regular salary along with a percentage of any excess commissions that are earned by him or her on a stipulated agreement with the agency. The insurance business is unique in that it allows most individuals to earn any amount of money that they desire, as long as they exert commensurate effort and can acquire the necessary technical and sales skill. Generally, there are many different salary-bonus arrangements. These will be discussd later.

A producer on pure commission is able to control his or her income level commensurate with efforts and sales ability, as long as he or she (1) has an equitable split of commission with the agency, and (2) has learned to budget the amount of commission received in a manner that will allow him or her to live as though he or she were being paid a salary. As every salesperson knows, there are high points, low points, and seasonal peaks in each business. In one month a salesperson can generate $10,000 in commissions and the next month $100,000. The successful producer, therefore, must learn to

Elements of Producer Compensation

spread the commissions in a manner that will reduce concerns about money.

Unless a producer has an existing book business or a sizeable savings account, it would be best not to enter the insurance business on a pure commission basis. Some plan for a draw against future commissions or a salary is recommended, along with a commission after a certain period or after a certain level of commission is reached. As a matter of interest a commission only arrangement ranked very low in importance to young producers who responded to a survey, discussed later, conducted by the Young Agents of Georgia.

Salary, whether straight salary, salary plus bonus, or pure commission is only one of the traditional elements of producer compensation. One must consider prerequisites that form the total compensation package. Obviously, if a producer is receiving a broad range of fringe benefits paid by the employer, he or she would be willing to take somewhat less in salary and/or commission, especially when one considers the tax advantages of employer funded plans. Also, the stage of the producer's career influences how important fringe benefits are in an overall compensation package. Initially, salary is the most important component of a producer's package. But as the producer matures, other benefits become more and more important.

Group Insurance

In addition to salary, the young producer needs other benefits to protect his or her financial security. Foremost among these is accident and sickness insurance. Group plans can vary from a basic hospital expense plan with a daily reimbursement limitation, to a so-called "comprehensive" plan that provides unlimited protection, subject to certain deductibles. The most important aspect of a group insurance plan is that it provides protection for catastrophic medical expenses which would otherwise create insolvency. Dental plans are becoming increasingly available for smaller groups; this could be extremely important for a young person with a growing family. Although currently the subject of some criticism from the Internal Revenue Service, medical reimbursement plans can be a valuable part of one's compensation program.

Life Insurance

Similarly, employer funded life insurance helps to provide financial security for a producer's family. Group life insurance can be purchased at extremely attractive rates, especially considering that it can be purchased with pre-tax dollars. Plans are generally designed so that an employee is provided with protection equal to a multiple of his or her salary or a certain amount for each year of service. A double indemnity provision may be placed on the coverage to double the benefit if death results from an accident. Or a separate accidental death and dismemberment policy can be purchased on a group basis. To complete the portfolio of group insurance fringe benefits, disability income should be provided to maintain the financial integrity of the family unit should the wage earner be disabled because of accident or sickness.

Automobile Expense

Unless a producer lives in a large metropolitan area with an excellent public transportation system, an automobile is an absolute necessity in the insurance business. Automobiles and associated expenses are becoming an ever-increasing component of the business budget, as well as the personal budget. Business related automobile expenses are deductible to the individual, as well as the firm.

Producer automobile expense is generally handled in one or two ways: (1) as a flat automobile expense allowance given to the producer on a monthly basis or (2) an automobile is provided for his or her use with associated expenses reimbursed by the agency. The advantage of an expense allowance is that the producer may select his or her own auto, depending on particular needs and life styles. Also, any excess business-related auto expenses may be deducted individually. Of course the advantage of a furnished automobile is that the producer incurs no auto expense. Technically, the IRS has ruled that if an employee is furnished a company automobile, that employee is required to declare as income, any nonbusiness mileage at the prevailing rate, or reimburse the company for this nonbusiness use (to and from the office is not considered business use).

Although an automobile is almost a necessity for the producer, it would be difficult to argue that the producer needs a Cadillac or Mercedes. In fact, it would be difficult for the agency to cost justify this type of expenditure. Yet the producer, may desire a larger and costlier auto in order to attract a certain segment of the market which the type of auto might impress (people like to do business with successful people). The producer in this situation, in order to obtain the expensive auto, should be willing to negotiate a reduced salary or commission to offset the cost of the auto or change to an auto expense allowance and purchase what he or she wishes.

Expense Accounts

Nearly all producers incur some sort of business related entertainment expense. Like automobile expense, business entertainment would be deductible either to the agency or the producer. Most agency's pay the producer for necessary expenses incurred to produce business in the form of an expense account, but, again, the method varies greatly between firms. Entertainment expense can be classified as: (1) direct entertainment expense and (2) indirect entertainment expense.

Direct sales expense, such as client business lunches, is normally reimbursable fully.

Indirect entertainment expense is somewhat more nebulous and would require a great deal more justification in order to be 100 percent deductible. The reason is that indirect sales expenses, in many cases, are not incurred for specific clients. These expenses instead, which include such items as country club dues, civic club dues, admission to athletic events, arts festivals, concerts and operas, and golf tournaments may enable the producer to establish prospects. Depending on the producer's individual life style, the agency paying for the producer's indirect business entertainment expenses could be very meaningful. In consideration for these benefits, paid by the agency, the producer may be willing to take less in salary or commission.

Vacations

The cost of a vacation is a personal, rather than a business expense. If paid by the company, the cost is deductible only if it can be shown to be a reasonable addition to compensation for services rendered. The producer would have to report it as income.

However, producers can combine business with vacation trips. For example, a producer in Atlanta may spend three days in San Francisco on a business trip, and then take a week's vacation in Aspen, Colorado. Here, the cost would have to be divided between the business element and the personal element. If the company pays for the entire trip, the cost of the personal element would have to be reported as income by the producer and could not be deducted by the company, unless considered to be additional compensation for services.

Education — Association Expense

It is certainly in the agency's best interest to provide its clients with proficient and capable producers not only to enhance the agency's reputation, but also to prevent possible errors and omissions. The agency should sponsor and encourage the producer to become involved in continuing education activities such as IIA, CPCU, CIC, and other product knowledge seminars. The agency also should bear the expense of these educational activities.

Similarly, by becoming involved with local, state and national insurance associations such as the Independent Insurance Agents of America or the Professional Insurance Agents, the producer gains a much broader prospective of how different agencies handle similar insurance problems. Association activities could be considered as a type of education expense, because they give the producer the benefit of other peoples' accomplishments which could be then implemented. Also, by uniting with other producers having similar problems, each has a better chance of getting problems solved, especially on the state or national level.

Retirement Plans

Part of everyone's long range goals includes the thought of eventually either discontinuing work altogether and retiring or reducing the workload in order to enjoy a semi-retired life style. Most people are unable to live comfortably on social security benefits alone. A retirement plan is certainly one of the more important prerequisites in a producer's overall compensation program.

Retirement plans take many forms and shapes ranging from a simple Keough Plan funded by life insurance to a Non-Qualified Income Continuation at Retirement Plan. Plans may be structured many different ways and use various financing vehicles. Despite the differences of plans one common characteristic of all plans is the sacrifice of certain current income for appreciation, subject to uncertain future income. The producer must be willing to make this commitment.

Employee Stock Option Plans

As discussed more fully later, employee stock option plans are an effective way to transfer limited ownership to producers as they become an increasing factor in the agency operation. Options may be granted at either below current market or the option price may be frozen for a definite period. From the agency's point of view, these plans can be an excellent tool to retain outstanding producers. To the producer, it is an easy and inexpensive way to acquire ownership in the firm and to provide long term security.

Intangibles

Aside from salary and benefits, both taxable and nontaxable, other areas that encompass a complete compensation program include mobility, public recognition and the environment in which the producer works. Mobility is difficult to measure, because it is more desirable to certain producers than to others. But what it encompasses is the individual's flexibility of office hours in order to accomplish the job. This can be extremely satisfying to experienced producers even though they do not own a portion of the agency. A second in-

Elements of Producer Compensation

tangible is public recognition. This is another important item that appeals more to the experienced producer, whether the recognition is from fellow producers who recognize certain accomplishments or by civic achievements. In order to be a successful producer, one must have an extremely strong ego. Another intangible is the environment in which the producer works, i.e., the office and surroundings. This is a benefit that lends itself to the producer's ego, because it provides a sense of status within the agency and makes for a more pleasant working environment.

CHAPTER 4

Relationship of Motivation to Producer Compensation

Any study of producer compensation must necessarily include the relationship of motivation to the compensation attained. Frederick Taylor's theory that individuals are primarily motivated by economic factors has been generally accepted, until recently. Motivation directly relates not only to performance, but also to the desired outcome of this performance, i.e., improved remuneration and feelings of accomplishment (job satisifaction). It is also a generally accepted fact that the individual must meet the basic needs before he or she can turn to the higher-order needs. Most theories support this idea. The very fact that the young producer has chosen a sales profession, indicates a motivation toward fulfilling some basic needs. This psychological need would be interpreted as a desire to be in a profession where there is much personal contact with others and a desire to feel superior. In explaining the products, the producer is, in reality, superior to the client who has no knowledge of the producer's field.

Motivation is necessary to success, because motivation actually means a person's need to act in a certain way. A person must be guided in the proper direction to perform in such a way as to guarantee positive accomplishments.

Motivational Factors

Presented here are five motivational factors for producer compensation levels.

Survival

As a basis of survival, a monthly salary based on such factors as previous experience, present book of business (if any), and the expectations of the employing agency should be provided. A guaranteed salary is essential for the basic needs of the new producer and his or her family, and may well be the means for survival until he or she begins to earn commissions. Not only is a basic salary mandatory for the needs of the family, but also for the young producer's peace of mind.

The producer will be better able to perform if the basic salary is large enough to provide for the family during the period that commissions may not be forthcoming. The agency employing a new young producer would be wise to provide a base salary large enough to enable the new producer to concentrate on his or her job performance without the worry that the basic needs of his or her family are in jeopardy.

Training of the new producer is essential. Office procedures must be learned to fit the individual agency needs.

Motivation As Factor of Compensation

Leads could be furnished and the company of another producer could be valuable from a motivational standpoint. The young producer should be encouraged to broaden his or her education by studying books and manuals. Attendance at seminars stressing sales procedures is helpful in learning not only sales openings and closings, but the psychological effect of sales techniques on potential clients. It is necessary for the producer during this period to become comfortable with what he and she is selling so that the effect of his or her sales presentations are acceptable. Insurance company schools for young producers are very valuable. They provide an atmosphere of learning where all the students are on the same educational level and give the young producer an opportunity to observe his and her peers. Such schools also give a feeling of competition which is essential to the chosen profession.

Security

As the young producer becomes experienced and his and her basic needs are being met, the producer will, if properly motivated by the forces mentioned in the foregoing paragraphs, begin to earn more money in the form of commissions. The need hierachy as developed by Abraham Maslow, prominent psychologist holds that motivation at the security level could be improved in several ways. One is the addition of more responsibility in the administration of the agency and in the marketing of accounts and becoming involved with company relations. Another possibly more important one is an increase in the base salary or commission.

A producer will generally perform at top level if he or she believes the result will be a successful performance resulting in financial gain. This is known as the effort-performance-reward linkage which consists of:

Producer Compensation

(1) Intrinsic rewards (related to the work itself and a feeling of accomplishment); and
(2) Extrinsic rewards (salary increases and/or better working conditions).

Frederick Herzberg stated that factors related to job content are motivators such as performing a job well and being praised. Thus, we see that when motivators are operative, the result is job satisfaction.

Job Satisfaction

The occupational level of a producer is an important influence. As a producer progresses up the organizational level, he or she is likely to achieve a strong feeling of job satisfaction. The structure of the organization also appears to be a factor, such as in an agency which permits the employees to satisfy their social needs and interact comfortably with each other and their superiors. The producer's flexible job structure also adds to this feeling of job satisfaction, particularly when the producer has the opportunity to schedule his or her own appointments and to have personal freedom concerning work schedules.

The producer's family also has an effect on his or her career. As the producer excels economically, the attitude of the family toward the bread winner is economic level and standing in the community are import factors. Active participation by the producer and spouse in religious, charitable or civic groups add to the overall satisfaction.

Fringe benefits of the job can add immensely to the satisfaction of both the producer and his or her family. A company car can release the family car for the use of the spouse. Health and accident insurance for the family at a reduced rate eases the worry over large unexpected medical expenses. A club membership or a company-owned resort, that can be utilized by employees helps to provide for recreation and vacation at reasonable costs. The agency that gives a bonus, provides a strong incentive for the young producer. If the agency offers profit sharing, this could be a decisive influence for the producer to remain with the agency on a long-term basis. An expense account can provide the producer with a feeling of trust and importance, too.

Esteem

Assuming that the producer has satisfied the basic needs, achieved some measure of security, and is satisfied with his or her job, McClelland's achievement theory would apply at this point. This theory is that some individuals have significantly higher need to achieve than others. The three distinct needs that are important are: the (1) need for achievement, (2) need for power and (3) need for affiliation. Maslow's esteem needs would also be germane at this time. The producer has a strong feeling of self-esteem and has the respect of his or her fellow workers, as well as of other people in the community. As his or her career progresses, the balance of needs change. If the producer attains financial security, self-esteem, the acceptance of others and a feeling of accomplishment all will satisfy the needs of his or her ego. However, the motivated person will pursue continuing education in order to widen his or her horizons. Education degrees can increase esteem from others and promote self-esteem.

Producer Compensation

Figure 1

NEED HIERACHY

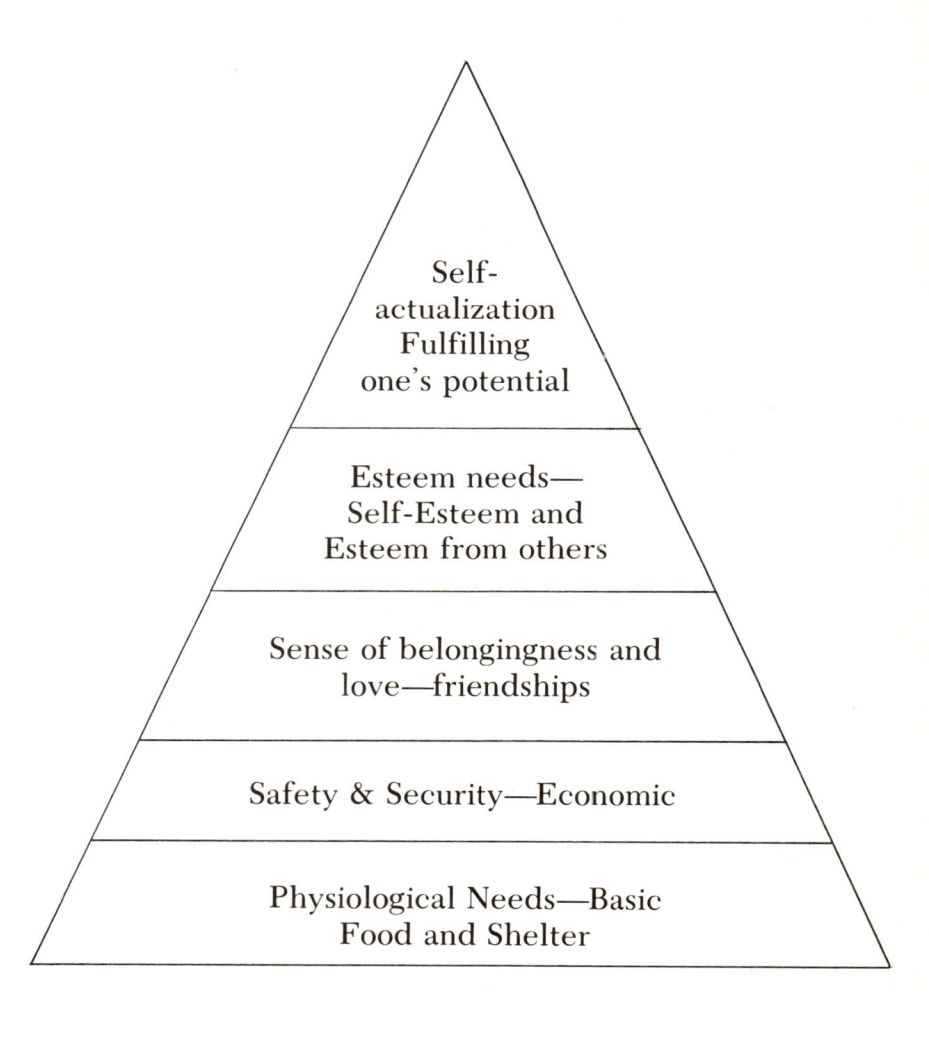

- Self-actualization Fulfilling one's potential
- Esteem needs—Self-Esteem and Esteem from others
- Sense of belongingness and love—friendships
- Safety & Security—Economic
- Physiological Needs—Basic Food and Shelter

Having met his or her basic needs, the producer will likely turn to safety and security needs. At this point the young producer must attain a financial status that will protect him or her and his or her family from economic disasters, and therefore a feeling of security regarding the profession. As the producer acquires more experience—and a feeling of competence, his or her feeling of security will increase. At this time the producer could begin to think of the job or profession as long term.

As Maslow's need hierachy is considered it can easily discern that the hiring agency will be able to satisfy the lower needs of the hierachy more than the top three, as illustrated in Figure 1.

Self Needs

As the producer reaches maturity, it should be his or her goal to reach the pinnacle of Maslow's theory by realizing full potential as a productive, creative person. If the goals of financial independence are achieved, either as a principal or as the owner of an agency, it can be assumed that the producer will also fulfill the needs to satisfy his or her feelings of personal worth and self-fulfillment. The complexity of individual needs is such, however, that a blanket statement such as the foregoing cannot be made to apply to each individual.

Survey Results

In order to test the importance of various compensation benefits and needs, The Young Agents Committee of the Independent Insurance Agents of Georgia conducted a survey with 134 young agents participating. The survey attempted to separate responses from owners, employed producers, and other agency personnel. In addition, there was a division by number of years a person had been employed in the agen-

Producer Compensation

cy business: 0-3 years, 4-10 years, and over 10 years. Nineteen items of compensation or fringe benefits were listed. The participants were asked to indicate the level of importance to each. The degrees of importance were: Very Important, Only Somewhat Important, Not Important at All, and Not Sure. Figure 2 provides a graphic look at the "very important" items ranked by percentages. A complete tabulation of the survey is found in Appendix A.

Of items indicated to be "Very Important," the most consistent were *job satisfaction, being able to realize one's full potential as a person, and ability to control one's income level. Ownership* (78 percent of owners responses) was "very important" more often to owners than employed producers.

Judging from these results one must conclude that various needs and benefits both tangible and intangible must be considered in order for a person to be attracted and retained in the insurance agency business.

COMPENSATION OR FRINGE BENEFITS INDICATED AS "VERY IMPORTANT"

Fig. 2

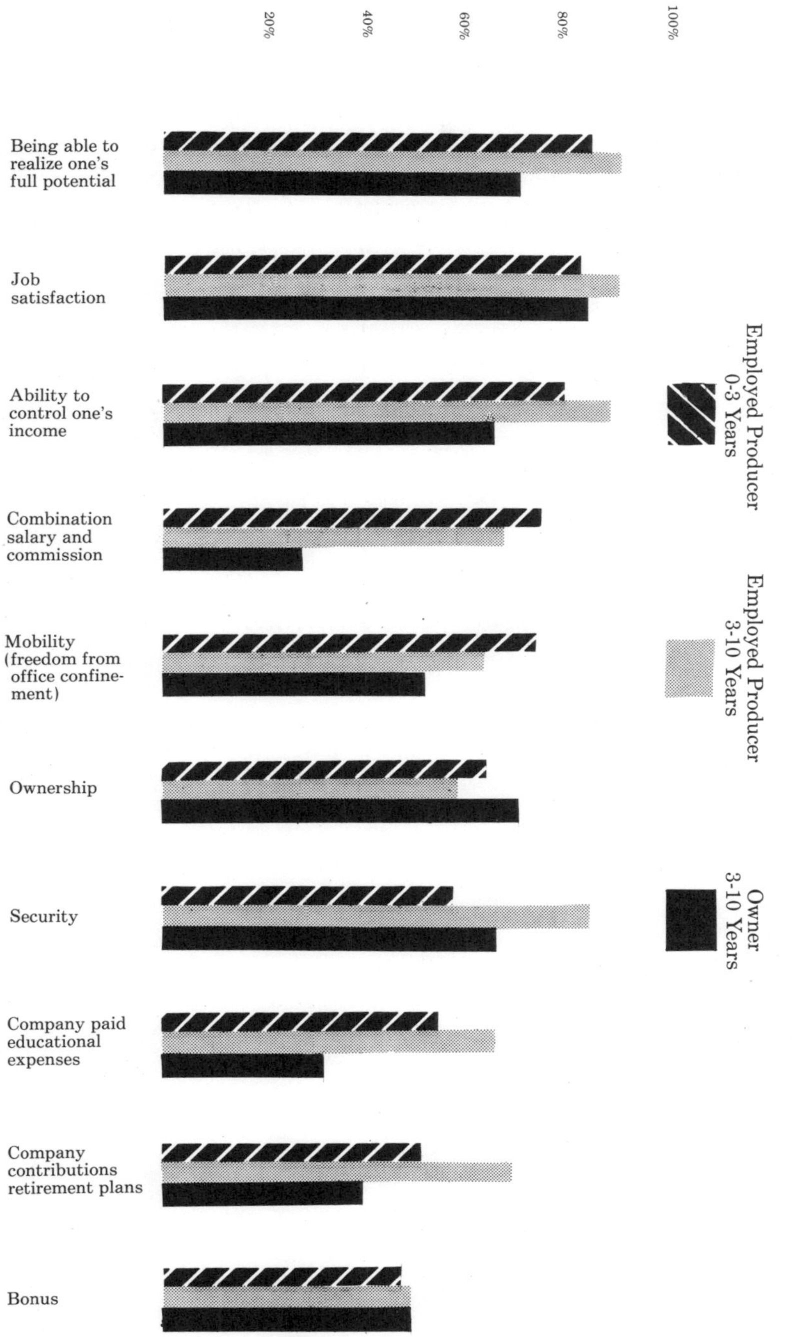
Employed Producer 0-3 Years
Employed Producer 3-10 Years
Owner 3-10 Years
20%
40%
60%
80%
100%
Being able to realize one's full potential
Job satisfaction
Ability to control one's income
Combination salary and commission
Mobility (freedom from office confinement)
Ownership
Security
Company paid educational expenses
Company contributions retirement plans
Bonus

20% 40% 60% 80% 100%

Company paid
life & health
insurance

Acceptance
from others

Expense
Account

Public
recognition

Transportable
skills

Salary
only

Commission
only

Club
membership

Company
car

CHAPTER 5

Agency Ownership

Ownership, a difficult topic for many producers to discuss, is equally elusive of simple definition. First, ownership may be active or inactive, or any combination thereof. Since the insurance business is a service business, inactive ownership offers few advantages, except to provide otherwise unavailable capital. However, it has many disadvantages and is usually best avoided.

Sole proprietorship, partnership and corporation are the three classes of ownership. The sole proprietor is normally the least prepared to effect ownership transfer to producers or family members. A partnership may consist of two or more persons who are active or inactive, equal or unequal, or general or limited partners. The death of one partner automatically, by operation law, dissolves the partnership. The surviving partner, as a liquidating trustee, is required to wind

Producer Compensation

up the business and pay net amounts to each surviving partner and the executor of the deceased partner. The surviving partner's only alternative is reorganization, if all surviving partners and heirs can agree. This might mean taking in the heirs as active or inactive partners. Or the surviving partners may sell out to the heirs or buy out their interests. While agreement is sometimes impossible, or at best difficult, the partnership at least offers a beginning point for orderly transfer of ownership.

A corporation may have one owner, many owners, or may even be publicly-owned. It is different from other forms of ownership, because it is a separate legal entity. Thus, when a stockholder dies or disposes of his or her stock, there is no legal effect on the corporations existence. Its life is usually perpetual and is effected only by its charter and state laws. While legal perpetuation is assured, little practical perpetuation may occur, if the heirs become the new owners. A one (active) owner corporation suffers most of the same problems as the sole proprietor. As inactive owners, heirs probably need income, derivable only as dividends, subject to dual income taxation. A conflict of interest often occurs because surviving stockholders, called upon to conduct the business alone, feel profits should go to them as salary or should be plowed back into the agency for future development. For another problem, heirs could decide to sell their stock to someone else. The corporation does, however, have significant advantages. One is the several classes of stock that can be made available.

Common stock is the type of stock normally carrying all rights of ownership. These rights include the right to vote, to participate in earnings, to maintain a percentage of ownership and to sell owned stock. Preferred stock, with more limited rights, is important in corporate ownership discussions. While it normally does not give rights to vote, it has preference or dividends on assets upon liquidation. The several types of preferred stock may be very useful to stop estate growth, since increase in values goes to common stock, even while protesting dividends (cumulative preferred is entitled to current and past dividends before common stock) and convertible preferred allows exchange to common to regain control of corporation if it should ever be necessary. Convertible bonds are not considered as direct ownership, but are generally exchangeable for common stock and may be used somewhat like preferred stock.

Ownership of expirations, personally produced business (or ownership of production), is an interesting form of internal agency ownership. It allows certain rights of a producer to that business personally produced.

Ownership As Motivation

Ownership contains elements of the best and worst of all worlds. It is about the best possible form of motivation, but it is fraught with dangers and, in the event of failure, has the most severe consequences. Once transferred, it is very hard to retrieve. The following discussion of ownership deals primarily with that traumatic transition that most agencies have either survived or must yet encounter: The evolution from a one-owner, one-manager agency to multiple ownership and divided responsibilities of management. The discussion is, however, generally applicable to all ownership transfers. Ownership should, and probably does, attract and retain better producers. In relation to Maslow's hierarchy of needs, ownership can motivate those successful to an extent beyond and above monetary need. A danger in multiple ownership (in the transition from single ownership), however, is it may be detrimental to central authority and

Producer Compensation

centralized control. It can destroy and divert consistent agency purpose and direction. Valuable time and effort can be spent solving differences of internal owners rather than selling and properly servicing insureds.

In fairness to everyone, any discussion of agency ownership should make mention of some of the advantages and disadvantages to both buyer and seller. For the seller, perpetuation may be the most important benefit. For the seller's protection and effective control, a majority of ownership may be maintained. A buy-sell agreement can protect the seller, and under certain conditions, allow him or her to regain a divested interest. Making producers owners, will help align producers goals and therefore make them consistent with that of the agency. It allows the seller to share management, possibly allowing more production time for the agency's most valuable producer.

With the needed buy-sell agreement, the seller faces a possibility of a new owner leaving at a bad time, causing the seller new estate problems and even cash flow problems, probably at a time when the seller is nearing retirement or at least thinking about it. Another problem is that expenses (such as for distant conventions) must be considered differently. Even a minority owner may build resentment if inequities remain. Another consideration is that the topnotch producer may not necessarily have management experience, personality or ability. He or she, therefore, may become a disruptive influence on the agency.

The new owner is offered an opportunity to participate in agency growth and profits and will begin to benefit from growth of in-house accounts. He or she should benefit from a proper buy-sell agreement just as the seller does; offering security of himself or herself and his or her family. Greater self-esteem and community status can result in personal

Agency Ownership

satisfaction and may actually directly help his or her sales efforts (particularly in a smaller community). A new minority owner, however, may find his or her rights and influence much weaker than anticipated, creating unhappiness and frustration. Paying for ownership may prove to be a problem and may drain needed family income at a bad time. New problems and inter-agency conflicts can disrupt an agency to everyone's financial and emotional detriment.

An alternative to outright ownership is the ownership by a producer of his or her personal production. While any percentage split is possible, 50% to each party is common. While ownership is normally on personally produced accounts, agency accounts given to producers for serving may be included. One such agreement allows growth to accrue to producers, but the original value of these accounts is deducted when business is bought back from producers. These agreements, usually written contracts, normally contain a vesting schedule, making them useful as a reward for long periods of service and preventing or allowing for vested interest while a producer is on a draw at the beginning of his or her career. Portability of producer business is sometimes allowed with producer buying agency half. An important consideration of allowing the producer to leave with business is market size. Impact in a small community would certainly be greater than in a large city and should be considered very carefully. Payment of 25% of the actual producer's commission or the agency's commission (if the producer is buying) for six years is a common price. Where this type of agreement is in effect, the actual annual producer commission may be reduced, since ownership in this fashion is obviously of value to a producer and should be considered in overall producer compensation.

While obviously not the same as full agency ownership,

ownership of production is an alternative for a producer if an owner refuses to sell. It can be useful where present ownership is inactive or nonproducing, since it acts to freeze growth in agency value. Freezing agency value can be an important consideration when an agency is in an estate or otherwise tied up for a long period. It is certainly worth considering in a family business as a means of motivation and reward based on revenue production instead of compensation primarily based on family relationship.

Transferring Ownership

When it comes to ownership transference, advice of a competent attorney and accountant is extremely important. Many of these methods require carefully executed documents. No one method works best for all circumstances, since estates (other financial interests and actual estate values) vary greatly and the human element (even competence) of those involved varies. Ownership is transferred through gifts and sales. Gifts, seemingly simple, are subject to annual tax exclusions, with the balance effecting estate tax deduction at the time of death by using the unified tax credit for gifts. Sales may be for cash or notes. In family transactions, in particular, notes may be carefully designed to be repaid from future earnings. Employee Stock Ownership Plans (ESOP) and Employee Stock Ownership Trusts (ESOT) are two relatively new devices that allow a selling owner to transfer ownership while retaining agency control. Stock options and stock redemptions are two possibilities worth consideration, too. The private annuity guarantees (if the agency remains solvent) a lifetime income to the seller and may be particularly useful in family situations. As previously mentioned, preferred stock is an effective way to transfer new growth in value of business to common

Agency Ownership

stockholders.

The two basic types of insurance agency ownership, outright agency ownership, and ownership of production, are not mutually exclusive, and in the case of family agencies, particularly may be used to accomplish several seemingly contradictory goals. One indisputable fact is that, with the exception of publicly-held agencies and those owned by holding companies or other businesses, change of ownership is inevitable. An orderly plan to transfer is certainly preferable, and when properly executed it can result in considerable tax savings.

CHAPTER 6

Developing A Producer Compensation Plan

This is an important chapter, because it deals with the practical application of the principles, goals, and objectives as discussed earlier in this text. It is simply the "how to" of developing a producer compensation plan. The objectives are to analyze the producer/principal relationship regarding needs, and desires of each over the career span of the producer, and to develop, through a systematic approach, a compensation package that meets the objectives of the principal and the producer.

Obviously, at any given time or stage in the career span of the producer/principal relationship, the needs, and desires of each person will vary. Because of this fact, certainly no one method is right for all. However, there are specific common components in all compensation arrangements, and a logical presentation of the thought process that relates all of these components is of primary importance. Illustrations are used to show practical application of the relationship between the common factors of compensation which are salary, commission, fringe benefits, bonuses, and ownership as they relate to the short, intermediate and long range goals of sound equitable producer compensation programs.

There are as many ideas, means, and methods of developing producer compensation programs, as there are individual agencies. These plans can run the gamut from a "sink-or-swim" to an "all-encompassing" plan that addresses itself to all factors of compensation.

Figure 3
SINK-OR-SWIM PLAN

Commission: 50% to 100% of first year commissions; renewals negotiable
Salary : None
Fringe Benefits : None
Bonus : None
Ownership : None

A producer—under a "sink-or-swim" plan as illustrated in Figure 3—is basically left to his or her own individual motivation and skills to determine the future, if the agency has no commitment to any of the factors of compensation. If the producer cannot develop an adequate commission level in a short period, he or she is likely to fail.

Developing a Compensation Plan

Figure 4
ALL-ENCOMPASSING PLAN

Commission	: 40% to 100% on new business 30% to 50% on renewal business
Salary	: New employees begin on a salary that terminates when commission income equals salary, or salary continues with a reduction in the commission percentage.
Fringe Benefits	: Possibilities include: automobile furnished or allowance given instead; life, health, disability, dental and medical reimbursement insurance plans, country club and civic club dues; qualified pension plan; profit sharing arrangements; expense accounts, paid vacations; savings and investment plans; educational course and self-improvement course fees; free parking, etc.
Bonus	: Possible arrangements: based on percentage of profits; performance of producer, if he or she exceeds goals (validation); Christmas bonus; contingent commission percentage; bonuses to be paid in lump sum annually, monthly or quarterly; bonuses based on percentage of gross commissions that increases every year; stock bonus trust, where agency gives stock as a bonus each year; or any other bonus.
Ownership	: Possibilities: employees stock ownership plans (ESOP); stock option based on preset formulas, number of years employed, or after validation for key or all producers.

Producer Compensation

In the opposite extreme, a compensation plan may encompass all of the factors of compensation, as shown in Figure 4, with a definite commitment from both the producer and the agency as to the success of both.

As one can see, the above type of plan offers the maximum commitment on the part of the producer/principal relationship to each other. All of the factors of compensation are used to develop security and motivation on the part of the producer, and a continued commitment to the success of the producer/principal relationship for the long term.

One must remember that the commission dollar can only be stretched so far for compensation purposes. At some point, the producer has to justify his or her economic existence. This point in time is of primary importance in the formulation of a compensation package, since the overriding factor in the producer/principal relationship is to make a profit.

Guesswork should not be the rule in determining what a producer should be paid. An agency should be able to identify precisely what producer and administrative costs are before it begins to formulate a compensation package for a producer. The question to be answered, of course, is just how much commission income must be produced to offset producer and administrative costs. The answer to this question, of course, is the break-even point, or that point where all producer and administrative costs have been met and at which no profit has been generated.

To understand producer costs, one must be able to identify and allocate expenses for each producer. Generally speaking, there are two categories of producer expense: direct sales expenses, and indirect sales expenses. Direct sales expenses are those costs such as, salaries, commissions, bonuses, car allowances, entertainment or any other ex-

Developing a Compensation Plan

penses allocated to the producer to generate a sale. Indirect expenses include all the other expenses allocated to the producer and generally take the form of some sort of a nonsales related expenses such as, retirement plans, group health plans, etc. In some cases, bad debts that may be charged to the producer depending on the agency philosophy may also be included.

Commission dollars not only pay for sales expenses, but also for administrative expenses—office salaries, utilities, taxes, rent, supplies, etc. The sum of the sales expenses plus the administrative expenses will equal the commission level needed to break even on a producer. Simply stated:

Sales Expense (Direct and Indirect) & Administrative Expense = Commission Income Needed to Break Even

Of course, any commission generated over the level needed to offset sales and administrative expenses is profit to the agency. The greater the profit percentage retained by management, the less commission dollars available to be used to compensate the producer, if administrative expenses remain constant.

A sound compensation program cannot be formulated unless one understands from one's financial statements what percentage of the agency commission dollar is going to adminstrative expenses and profit. If these percentages are known, one can then determine what percentage of that commission dollar should go to the producer.

Short Range Goals

Zero to Three Years

As illustrated in Figures 3 and 4, there is an immense differential between the two compensation package extremes. Most compensation plans will tend to fall somewhere in between. The question to answer at this stage is how to go

Producer Compensation

about developing a compensation package, when there is such a great latitude to work within.

To help one answer this question, Chapter 1 suggested that the career span of a producer could be divided into three distinct time periods, and that the goals and objectives of the producer/principal relationship change during these distinct time periods; i.e., short range goals (0-3 years), intermediate range goals (3-10 years), and long range goals (10 years-retirement). Even if one accepts the premise of dividing the career span in this manner, it must first be realized that any compensation program must be able to fit within the budgetary allowances of one's individual agency's financial status. Also, even within these career divisions, logic would dictate that the age, experience, and present economic position of the new producer would have an effect on the compensation plan offered.

The thought process in developing a compensation program for the important first three years of a new producer's career first, requires that relative importance of each of the compensation factors be determined, as they relate to each individual producer's needs, wants, desires, and experience level.

The producer should expect a reasonable and equitable income based on his or her performance. Such performance is a direct result of the degree of motivation and the application of the person's training. The new producer should be aware of the fundamental requisite, that, if he or she meets or exceeds the level of performance expected, he or she will have the chance of increased income in the future. As income increases, the opportunity for increased responsibilities and the opportunity for advancement will follow, as determined by each individual agency's philosophy.

Since the first three years will generally determine

Developing a Compensation Plan

whether a new producer has the qualities needed to be successful, or whether or not the agency environment is compatible with his or her personality, it is important to determine which compensation factors are of the most importance. Emphasis should be placed on those most important factors initially, with the other factors being reserved for the intermediate and long range goals.

It can be held to be logically factual that the most important factors of compensation for a new producer are those that will help him or her maintain his or her present standard of living, while building a foundation for an economic future. In other words, commission, salary, or a combination of the two, are of primary importance at this time. Fringe benefits, bonuses, and ownership are of importance, of course, but are generally not as important as direct income to the producer during the first three years.

Now, what kind of commission, salary, or combination should be used? It can generally be concluded that, unless a new producer is being hired from another experienced selling environment, a commission only arrangement is dangerous for the first three years. The reason, obviously, is that if the producer does not produce enough commission to maintain his or her present standard of living, he or she may become disenchanted. This could have the unwanted result of forcing producers who develop slowly out of the industry.

Producer Compensation

Figure 5
COMMISSION ONLY PLAN

Commission:	50% to 100% new business
	40% to 60% renewals
Salary	: None
Fringe Benefits	: Car, life and health insurance, club dues
Bonus	: 5% of gross commissions
Ownership	: None

The type of arrangement illustrated in Figure 5 can be offset through the use of some type of commissions against a draw, as shown in Figure 6, or a salary against a draw program that gives the producer more security and stability. Under one of these types of plans, the producer is paid an agreed upon salary or is permitted to retain an agreed upon percentage of the commissions earned, subject to repayment, if the producer fails to meet pre-determined objectives (validation). The type of plan that offers a draw can be simple with implied objectives, or it can be formalized with its degree of formality limited only to the imagination of the program designer.

Developing a Compensation Plan

```
            Figure 6
       COMMISSION/DRAW PLAN

Commission: $15,000 draw to be negotiated annually
Salary     : None
Fringe
Benefits   : Car, life and health insurance, club dues
Bonus      : 50% of excess of validation
Ownership  : None
```

The plan that offers the most stability and security to a new producer is a salary only plan, as shown in Figure 7. The salary is large enough to support a required standard of living. This type of plan does not require the producer to repay anything to the principal, if the producer does not succeed. Generally, the basis of salary depends on the level of the producer's experience.

```
            Figure 7
       SALARY ONLY PLAN

Commission: None
Salary     : $15,000 to $22,000, subject to annual
             negotiation
Fringe
Benefits   : Car, life and health insurance, club dues
Bonus      : Based on percentage of agency profit
Ownership  : None
```

Producer Compensation

A plan might use both commission and salary arrangements to offer stability, as well as additional motivational qualities to the producer, such as shown in Figure 8.

Figure 8
COMBINATION COMMISSION AND SALARY PLAN

Commission and Salary:
- 1st year — $18,000
- 2nd year — 100% commission
- 3rd year — 75% commission
- 4th year and thereafter — 50% commission

Fringe Benefits : Car, life and health insurance, club dues

Bonus : Based on percentage of profit developed by each producer

Ownership : None

The combination of salary and commission arrangement, as shown in Figure 8, can be extended even further to a predetermined sales expense percentage of the commission dollar through the use of a formal validation schedule, based on the hypothetical optimum of the commission dollar being divided as follows:

Administration Expense	—	45%
Sales Expense	—	35%
Profit	—	20%
Total Commission Dollar	—	100%

Developing a Compensation Plan

Figure 9
VALIDATION SCHEDULE

Monthly salary $1,000		—	$12,000
Payroll taxes, group insurance, auto allowance, profit sharing, etc.		—	6,900
Sales Expense		—	$18,900

Validation Commission = $54,000
($54,000 x 35% = $18,900.)
($54,000 x 45% = $24,300.)
($54,000 x 20% = $10,800.)

Monthly Salary	Validation Commission	Bonus Percentage on Commission in Excess of Validation
$1,000	$ 54,000	35%
1,100	58,000	35%
1,200	62,000	35%
1,300	66,000	35%
1,400	70,000	35%
1,500	74,000	35%
1,600	78,000	35%
1,700	82,000	35%
1,800	86,000	35%
1,900	90,000	35%
2,000	94,000	35%
2,100	98,000	35%
2,200	102,000	35%
2,300	106,000	35%
2,400	110,000	35%

Figure 9 offers a formalized cost effective approach to a producer compensation plan, where all compensation is predicted on 35 percent of the commission dollar income. The actual percentage of the total commission dollar applied to each division will, of course, vary depending upon individual agency philosophy, efficiency, and management effectiveness.

Intermediate Range Goals

Three—Ten Years

Once a producer has proven himself or herself and has justified the ability to make a profit for the agency, the needs, and desires of the producer/principal relationship change. Usually, this will occur during the second phase of the producer's career span. At this point the producer is a functioning integral part of the agency profit picture.

The principal at this time has usually made a commitment to the producer and wants to continue the relationship. In addition to a satisfactory compensation arrangement, the principal must also remember that motivation of the producer is of prime importance. The producer must continue to be given good working conditions, good leadership and guidance, compassion during the hard times, and praise during the good times. The principal should also place continued emphasis on sound training and professionalism to round out the qualities of the producer. Also, about this time, the producer should be offered an opportunity of increased responsibilities and participation in agency affairs, if he or she so desires.

In this intermediate phase, the factors of compensation should be focused upon in a different light, because they take on different meanings to the producer. Obviously, the

Developing a Compensation Plan

producer is concerned with his or her direct income either through commission, salary, or a combination of the two. Fringe benefits, bonuses, and ownership become increasingly more important, too.

The principal may want to continue the original compensation plan for the producer, but it is important at this time to offer the producer a means to increase his or her income dependent upon performance and balanced for any additional responsibilities given the producer. Fringe benefits should carry more importance and should possibly be broadened to add to the stability and security of the producer, as well as contain continued motivational qualities. Bonus possibilities should continue to add impetus for increased sales, and ownership considerations should be given to those who are deemed worthy by the principal in order to wed those individuals to the organization.

One such program that addresses itself to the qualities of such a program during the intermediate stage of the producer's career is as illustrated in Figure 10.

Producer Compensation

Figure 10
INTERMEDIATE STAGE COMPENSATION PLAN

Commission: None

Salary : Based on commission income handled with additional compensation for percent of increase over previous years, new production, bad debts, accounts receivable, expenses, percentage of expenses, etc.

Fringe
Benefits : Car, life and health insurance, disability plan; social and civic club dues; paid vacations; profit sharing plan

Bonus : 10% of annual salary if pre-set goals are exceeded

Ownership : Option to buy stock after five years in service

Long Range Goals

Ten Years to Retirement

Last phase in the career span of the producer covers the greatest amount of time. It is the period between 10 years in the business until retirement. However, it is a less volatile period than the first two time periods. Obviously, if a producer stays employed by the same agency longer than ten years, he or she is not likely to leave, unless circumstances change drastically.

As the producer ages, his or her prospective on life and career change accordingly. Stability and security are again

Developing a Compensation Plan

key words, but increased income is not always a motivational factor after many years as a producer. There are certain intangibles that a person aspires to in order to feel that he or she has made a contribution to the agency and to society, as a whole. These intangibles will certainly vary from person to person, but nonetheless have to do with a feeling of self-fulfillment.

The producer may obtain this fulfillment through obtaining professional status; e.g., CPCU, CLU, CIC, etc.; through involvement in local, state, and national insurance activities or through ownership in the agency. No matter what method is used, financial success is still not enough for most people. There must be a feeling of self-esteem before a career can be complete.

During this last segment of the producer/principal relationship, the principal must look also to the long range goals he or she has set for himself or herself and the producer. The principal must decide what to do in the event he or she develops sickness, disability or death. He or she must also have long range objectives concerning agency perpetuation with commitment to those objectives.

One might ask the question, why would an agency want to perpetuate itself in the first place. Most principals have enough ego to want to continue the existence of his or her individual business philosophy, which is the result of many years of trial and error, and is permeated with his or her own individual style. The principal will also want to protect the assets of the agency that have taken so many years to acquire, and to continue the public image and confidence that has developed through so much hard work. In summation, the principal wants to insure that his or her efforts are not wasted.

To promote agency perpetuation, the long range goals of

Producer Compensation

the producer compensation program should focus on those factors of compensation that facilitate this end. Direct income becomes not as important as providing the producer with some means of ownership, so that the producer now becomes a principal and has a voice in the philosophy of the agency. The producer's compensation should reflect his or her ever-increasing role in agency management and ownership. Hence, agency titles, e.g., Vice President, etc., and overall increases in all factors of compensation become important. Specifically, the factors of fringe benefits, bonuses, and ownership are primarily important.

Figure 11 depicts a possible compensation plan that could be used during this period. The ultimate plan would be a combination of the benefits outlined earlier in Figure 4.

Figure 11

LONG RANGE COMPENSATION PLAN

Commission	: None
Salary	: Based on percentage of commissions earned, responsibilities within agency, and increase over previous year.
Fringe Benefits	: Car furnished; life and health insurance, disability, dental, and medical reimbursement plans; country clubs and civic club dues; qualified pension plan; profit sharing arrangement; expense accounts, paid vacations, and possible savings and investment plans.
Bonus	: Up to 10% of pre-tax income.
Ownership	: Stock options financed by agency at low interest rates.

Conclusion

As stated in this chapter, there are as many different compensation plans as there are agencies. This chapter has given the reader some insight into components that form producer compensation plans, and how they relate to the *short, intermediate,* and *long range objectives* of the producer/principal relationship. Readers should be able to combine the information given in this chapter with their own personal and agency objectives to formulate an equitable, flexible, and economically feasable compensation plan for their agency.

CHAPTER 7

Auxiliary Staff Functions

Producing business is not the only career path one may follow in today's modern insurance agency. With increasing complexity of the insurance business and greater demand on the producer's time, many agencies have added auxiliary staff functions to facilitate increased production or business.

Other career paths that a young person may elect to follow are *agency marketing management* (agency placer), *underwriting management, claims management,* and *administrative or service management.* As has been suggested in the previous chapters, the size and age of the agency determines the necessity for implementing various programs. There may be several people or a department serving one of these auxiliary staff functions in a large agency, and, conversely, in a small agency one person could serve two or more of these

Producer Compensation

functions. For purposes of this subject, all of these functions are combined under the title, underwriting manager, even though each of the above functions would support a unique career path.

It is difficult to design a compensation program for the auxiliary staff of an agency, because its impact on agency profits cannot be directly measured, unlike that of the producer. Most auxiliary staff personnel are paid on a straight salary basis or salary and bonus. However, in order to maintain upward mobility, an effective method should be devised to measure over contribution in concrete terms.

Clearly, there are distinct benefits to the agency that employs an underwriting manager. Foremost among these is more effective use of the producer's time, and hence, increased production. The question that agency principals must ask themselves, when contemplating the addition of an auxiliary staff manager is whether it will be cost effective in terms of increased growth to the agency.

Hand in hand with the plan for growth is the decision of the agency principals that growth is wanted, and that the underwriting manager is a key to that growth. Without this decision by the principals, the total package of expenses for the underwriting manager will seem too large. In most cases, this is the first position that the agency will consider to represent a total minus figure to the agency's balance sheet. The commitment by the principals will also be needed to help give the underwriting manager the support needed to make changes in the personal and commercial lines department. These changes sometimes are difficult to make and would be impossible without the support of principals.

There are specific reasons for wanting to become an underwriting manager. As stated earlier, there are several motivating factors that may attract someone to the American

Auxiliary Staff Functions

Agency System. Some of these include *excellent pay, possible ownership*, and *management potential*. All of these factors have a role in attracting an underwriting manager to the agency business. However, another factor that may carry more weight, in convincing someone to become an underwriting manager is "career stimulation motivation."

Insurance companies are often too slow in identifying their key underwriters and in promoting them. Because the necessary stimulus is not provided, these underwriters may become "stale" and may eventually lose the necessary attributes for writing good business. For the underwriter who feels "fenced in" and experiences loss of motivation, the position of underwriting agency manager may provide both the motivation and stimulation needed to fulfill his or her career aspiration.

At the company level, the underwriter may be responsible for work processed by employees working with him or her, but may have little input into the direction the company may take. An underwriting agency manager, on the other hand, not only will be responsible for the department, but also will participate in corporate decisions that will determine how the agency can grow, whether by merger or acquisition.

The underwriting agency manager is also charged with the responsibility to provide markets for the accounts obtained by the producers. This means that, instead of looking at an account and deciding whether it meets the insurance companies' guide lines, the underwriting agency manager determines, instead, what market will be the best, considering price, coverage, and availability. The underwriting manager is encouraged to use all of his or her resources for the benefit of the agency, as opposed to being "fenced in" by insurance company guide lines.

Agencies interested in employing an underwriting manager have more limited sources from which to obtain their prospects than would be the case when prospecting for a producer. One possible source for an underwriting manager is from another agency. Both standard and excess and surplus lines insurance companies are another possible source. Present agency producers may also be interested in trying their hand at underwriting. However, such person would be required to have product/coverage knowledge which is essential for the position.

This discussion thus far has dwelled on the position of underwriting agency manager as an all-inclusive position. As will be discussed later, there are varying opinions on what this person should do in that capacity and how much he or she should be paid. By using different job titles for the position, the agency may be able to establish a career path.

Benefits

Having determined that an underwriting manager is necessary, and having filled that position, the agency can benefit in a number of ways.

One of these benefits is that someone now officially has the responsibility and authority to handle matters of importance that otherwise would have been done by other individuals who may not have been as proficient in handling the underwriting and placing of business. By being given the responsibility for underwriting and placing business, the underwriting manager makes it his or her business and obligation to stay current with the markets and the new products available from the agency's companies. It should also be the manager's responsiblity to report suggestions for new companies to the principal. By having better information about the markets, the agency may spend less money "spinning its wheels," by not giving applications to companies where the risks do not meet the company's prime underwriting guidelines.

Another benefit to the agency is an organized underwriting department to assist the agency in processing its business. By providing cross training to the personnel that handle all types of business, the producer is assured that the policy being delivered to the customer is correct in premium and in coverage. Through the combination of these two benefits, the agency is able to grow larger because the underwriting and production departments are free to prospect and solicit new business.

Thus, without the efforts of an underwriting manager, the growth of an agency may be slower, more expensive and could require more effort from everyone.

Responsibilities

Although the responsibilities of a commercial lines manager can be similar in many ways to the responsibilities of a personal lines manager, the remainder of this chapter concentrates on the former—which was the subject of this study. Explored here are the duties and responsibilites of the commercial lines manager in three situations. The first is when there is an absence of a formal commercial lines department. The second is when a formal commercial lines department exists in the agency. And, the third situation is when the placement of business is a responsibility that is divided between the manager and others.

No Formal Commercial Lines Department

In a situation when an agency has no formal commercial lines department, but the work is performed through the guidance of a commercial lines manager, that person's

Producer Compensation

responsibilities are likely to entail the following:
- A. Placing and underwriting new and renewal business as requested by the producer.
- B. Keeping records of submissions sent to the agency's companies.
- C. Designing the agency's proposal format.
- D. Maintaining information on all markets available to the agency.
- E. Maintaining the communication line between producers and agency management.
- F. Assisting in company evaluations, i.e., product line and pricing.
- G. Supervising employees of the department, including salary administration, vacations, etc.

Effect of Formal Commercial Lines Department

When an agency has a formal commercial lines department, the department generally is responsible to the commercial lines manager for checking on all business produced by the agency, whereas the commercial lines manager is responsible for the everyday administration of personnel, and the following:
- A. Placing, pricing and underwriting new and renewal business.
- B. Keeping records of submissions sent to the agency's companies.
- C. Designing agency surveys, application and proposal formats.
- D. Maintaining information on the agency's markets, both standard and nonstandard.
- E. Maintaining lines of communication between producers and agency management.
- F. Assisting in agency growth by investigating new com-

Auxiliary Staff Functions

panies, new market approaches, and evaluating the results.
G. Establishing, administrating and training personnel of the commercial lines department, including salary, vacation and other employee benefits.
H. Working with producers on presentation of proposals to special clients.

A Divided Responsibility

Sometimes the commercial lines manager does not handle all of the placement of business, and the commercial lines department does not perform all of the functions that are necessary in processing commercial lines business. In a situation such as this, the commercial lines manager may only be responsible for:
A. Underwriting new business and assisting the producers in placement of some accounts.
B. Designing the agency's application.
C. Maintaining information for the agency's producers concerning markets.
D. Maintaining communication between producers and agency managers.
E. Providing input into agency goal formulation.
F. Supervising commercial lines department personnel.

In cases where there is divided responsibility, the commercial lines manager is likely to be freed of having to keep formal records on the agency's submissions to its companies, and in the administration of personnel.

Methods of Remuneration

Since there are different responsibilities of the commercial lines manager, there are different ways to remunerate him or her. The following are some of the more common

Producer Compensation

ways to reward the services of the commercial lines manager (and the personal lines manager if an agency has one).

Salary-Bonus-No Contract

The commercial lines manager receives a salary, along with a bonus based on the agency's production goal. The position involves no contract, and therefore, there is no formal arrangement for ownership in the agency.

Compensation includes standard medical and life insurance paid by the agency, a company expense account including all expenses for education. But no automobile is provided.

Salary-Non Related Bonus-No Contract

The commercial lines manager is on salary with a bonus that is not connected to agency growth or underwriting profits. There is no formal contract, but future purchase of ownership in the agency is available, but not guaranteed.

Compensation includes maintenance and use of a company auto, expense account, standard medical and life insurance benefits, and educational expenses, but no formal retirement plan.

Auxiliary Staff Functions

Salary-Production Bonus-Contract

The commercial lines manager is on a salary, plus monthly production bonus. The production goal is established and, if net, provides a specific amount of bonus. If the goal is exceeded, there is an amount established for each increment over the goal. Also, the manager is under a contract with a noncompete clause.

Compensation includes standard medical and life insurance benefits, education expenses, expense account and an auto allowance but no auto is furnished.

Salary-Contract-No Bonus or Ownership

The commercial lines manager is on a salary basis only with no bonus arrangement. In addition, a contract with a noncompete clause applies, but there is no provision for ownership or equity in the agency.

Compensation includes standard medical and life expenses, company auto, education expenses, and a retirement plan.

Producer Compensation

> ### Salary-Contract With Profit Sharing Bonus And Equity Arrangement
>
> The commercial lines manager is on a salary. Also a contract applies that includes a noncompete clause, profit sharing bonus and equity retirement arrangement. The profit sharing is tied to production underwriting results. A percentage arrangement is worked out between the commercial lines manager and the principal of the agency.
>
> The principle behind the equity retirement arrangement is that, as the commercial lines commission income increases to pre-determined levels, the manager receives a set percentage of that commission income when he or she retires.
>
> Compensation includes standard medical and life expenses, education expenses, company auto with certain limitations, and an expense account. There is no formal retirement.

Despite the various compensation plans that are available, there is no one plan that is the best. Each should be tailored to the circumstances. One of the interesting points learned during the survey was that all commercial lines managers interviewed preferred a form of compensation based on either (1) underwriting profits, (2) agency growth, or (3) a combination of the two.

CHAPTER 8

The Time Line of An Insurance Agency

    This chapter traces the growth of the ABC Insurance Agency over a 20-year period, beginning in 1981 when the agency was a sole proprietorship, the owner was 45 years old, and the premium volume was $550,000.

    The objectives of the owner are to retire in the year 2000 when he is 65 years old, be the majority stockholder and have about $800,000 in equity. In order to meet this goal, the owner realizes that the premium income must grow and that additional producers must be added in some planned manner.

    During 1981, the owner hires his first producer, referred to her as producer 1981A. This producer is to be paid a salary with an equity option in 1983. For an illustration of the changes in ownership see Tables 1 and 2.

Producer Compensation

TABLE 1
THE ABC INSURANCE AGENCY
Income Statement
For Year Ended December 31, 1981

Agency Premium	$550,000
Property/Casualty and other income	104,500
Office and General Expense	45,564
Total Sales Expense	13,688
Compensation to Owner	45,248

Producer 1981A joined agency during the Year 1981 with equity option at Year 1983.

OWNERSHIP (Valued at 1.5 times income)

STOCKHOLDER	**VALUE**	**PERCENTAGE**
Original Owner	$156,750	100%

Time Line of An Agency

TABLE 2
THE ABC INSURANCE AGENCY
Income Statement
For Year Ended December 31, 1983

Agency Premium	$850,000
Property/Casualty and other income	159,553
Office and General Expense	71,000
Total Sales Expense	20,423
Compensation to Owners	68,129

Producer 1981A exercised option to purchase stock during the Year 1983.

OWNERSHIP (Valued at 1.5 times income)

STOCKHOLDER	VALUE	PERCENTAGE
Original Owner	$198,039	82.7%
Producer 1981A	41,289	17.3
Total	$239,328	100.0%

The agency experiences "real growth" of approximately 13% annually. For simplicity the owner decides to value the ABC Insurance Agency at 1.5 times the annual income. In addition, he makes available stock ownership to each deserving producer after a minimum of three years employment with the agency.

We now look at the agency in 1985 as the premium volume increases to $1,500,000. In setting his objectives, the original owner intended to bring in new producers as they are needed. He now decides to bring in Producer 1985B, his second addition, who brings some business with him. Producer 1985B is paid a salary and is guaranteed an equity option, but only after 5 years with the agency. Refer to Table 3 for the

Producer Compensation

changes in ownership affecting the original owner and producer 1981A.

TABLE 3
THE ABC INSURANCE AGENCY
Income Statement
For Year Ended December 31, 1985

Agency Premium	$1,500,000
Property/Casualty and other income	279,888
Office and General Expense	124,826
Total Sales Expense	41,144
Compensation to Owners	113,918

Producer 1985B joins agency during the Year 1985 with an equity option at Year 1990.

OWNERSHIP (Valued at 1.5 times income)

STOCKHOLDER	VALUE	PERCENTAGE
Original Owner	$288,291	68.6%
Producer 1981A	131,540	31.4
Total	$419,831	100.0%

Table 4, shows the agency producing income of $549,720. Producers 1990C and 1990D contributed to this increase in income by their additional business. Producer 1990C was promised an equity option for 1995 after 5 years of service, whereas producer 1990D does not desire any equity in lieu of a larger salary. Producer 1985B exercises his equity option thereby becoming the third owner.

Time Line of An Agency

TABLE 4
THE ABC INSURANCE AGENCY
Income Statement
For Year Ended December 31, 1990

Agency Premium	$3,000,000
Property/Casualty and other income	549,720
Office and General Expense	246,275
Total Sales Expense	93,452
Compensation to Owners	209,993

Producer 1985B exercised his option to purchase stock during the year.

Producer 1990C added during the year with equity option for year 1995.

Producer 1990D added during the year also with no equity option.

OWNERSHIP (Valued at 1.5 times income)

STOCKHOLDER	VALUE	PERCENTAGE
Original Owner	$490,665	59.5%
Producer 1981A	232,727	28.2
Producer 1985B	101,187	12.3
Total	$824,579	100.0%

Table 5 reflects the income statement with ownership changes in the year 1995. Producer 1990C exercised his stock option, thus, becoming the fourth owner. An additional producer, 1995E, was hired during the year with no promise of any stock ownership for the future.

Producer Compensation

TABLE 5
THE ABC INSURANCE AGENCY
Income Statement
For Year Ended December 31, 1995

Agency Premium	$4,750,000
Property/Casualty and other income	868,312
Office and General Expense	389,754
Total Sales Expense	174,649
Compensation to Owners	303,909

Producer 1990C exercised his option and purchased stock.

Producer 1995E added during the year with no equity option.

OWNERSHIP (Valued at 1.5 times income)

STOCKHOLDER	VALUE	PERCENTAGE
Original Owner	$729,609	56.0%
Producer 1981A	352,199	27.0
Producer 1985B	160,923	12.3
Producer 1990C	59,736	4.7
Total	$1,302,467	100.0%

The ABC Insurance Agency, in the year 2000, shows a much larger operation than the one that existed during the first formal planning year, 1981. The premium volume increased from $550,000 to $6,000,000, the number of owners has grown from one to four and the equity has multiplied from $156,750 to $1,470,764.

Let's look at the original owner: He is now 65 years old and ready to retire. His total compensation has increased steadily over the last 20 years. He has brought in three other

Time Line of An Agency

producers, 1981A, 1985B, and 1990C, who are now ready to take over completely running the agency. He has achieved his objective of equity in excess of $800,000 knowing that without the additional people this would probably not have been possible.

TABLE 6
THE ABC INSURANCE AGENCY
Income Statement
For Year Ended December 31, 2000

Agency Premium	$6,000,000
Property/Casualty and other income	980,510
Office and General Expense	451,062
Total Sales Expense	191,211
Compensation to Owners	338,296

There are no new producers brought into the agency during the year nor stock options granted to new producers.

OWNERSHIP (Valued at 1.5 times income)

STOCKHOLDER	VALUE	PERCENTAGE
Original Owner	$813,758	55.3%
Producer 1981A	394,273	26.8
Producer 1985B	181,960	12.3
Producer 1990C	80,773	5.6
Total	$1,470,764	100.0%

See Figure 12 on *Agency Premium* and Figure 13 on *Total Compensation To Owners* for a graphic look at the changes over the 20 year period. Figure 14 on *Owners' Equity* shows the original owner's equity as a relationship to the equity new stockholders.

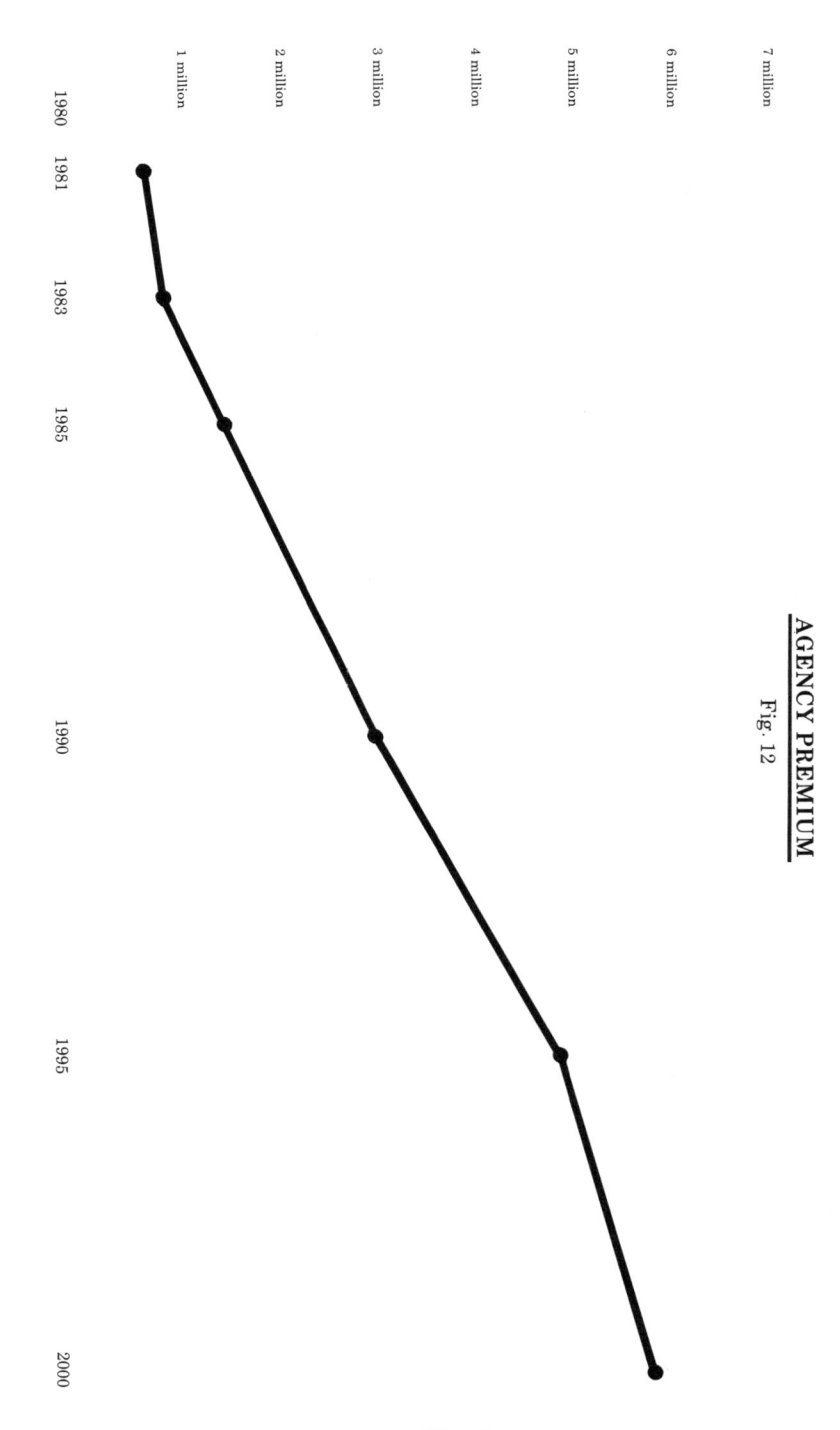

AGENCY PREMIUM
Fig. 12

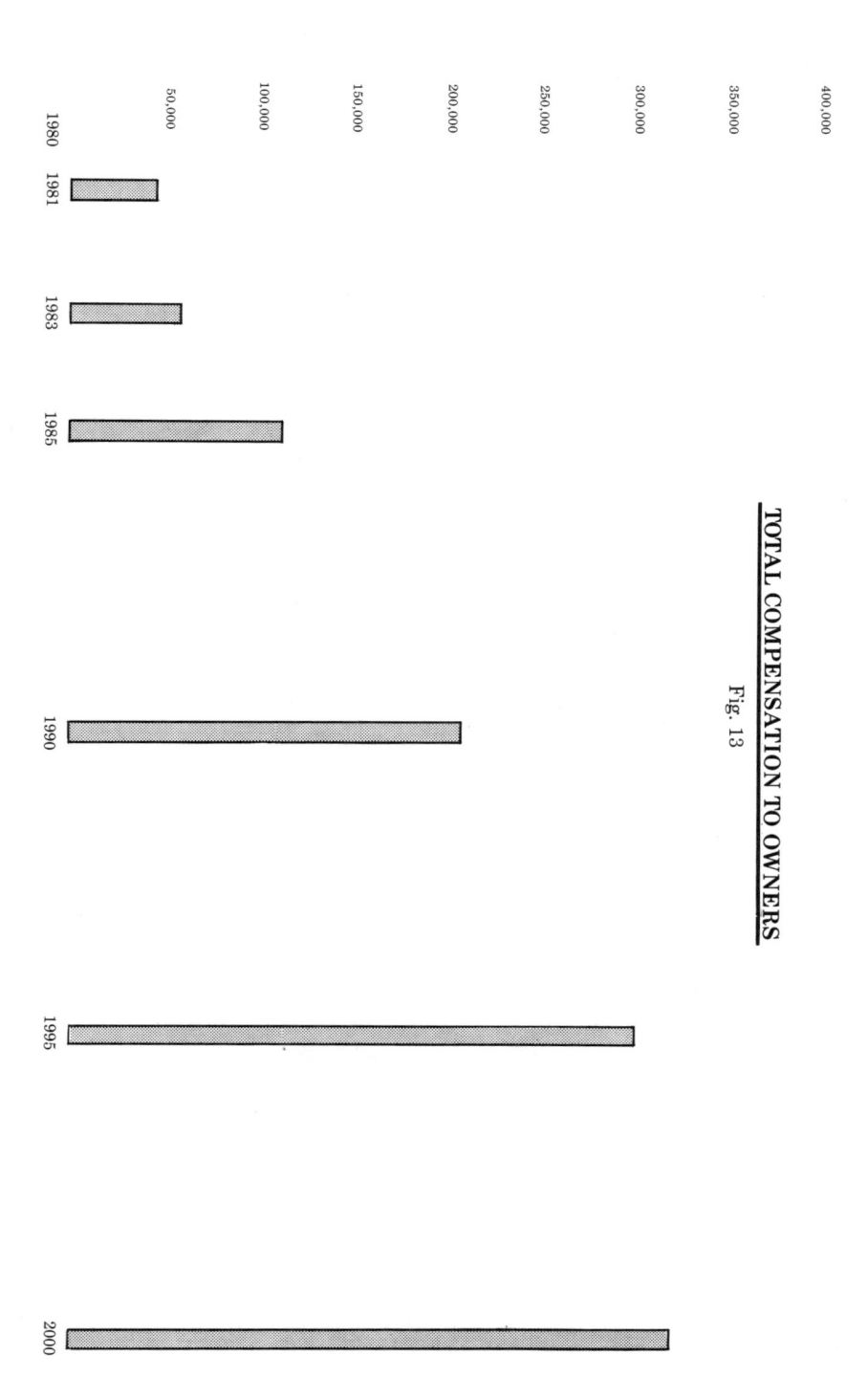

TOTAL COMPENSATION TO OWNERS

Fig. 13

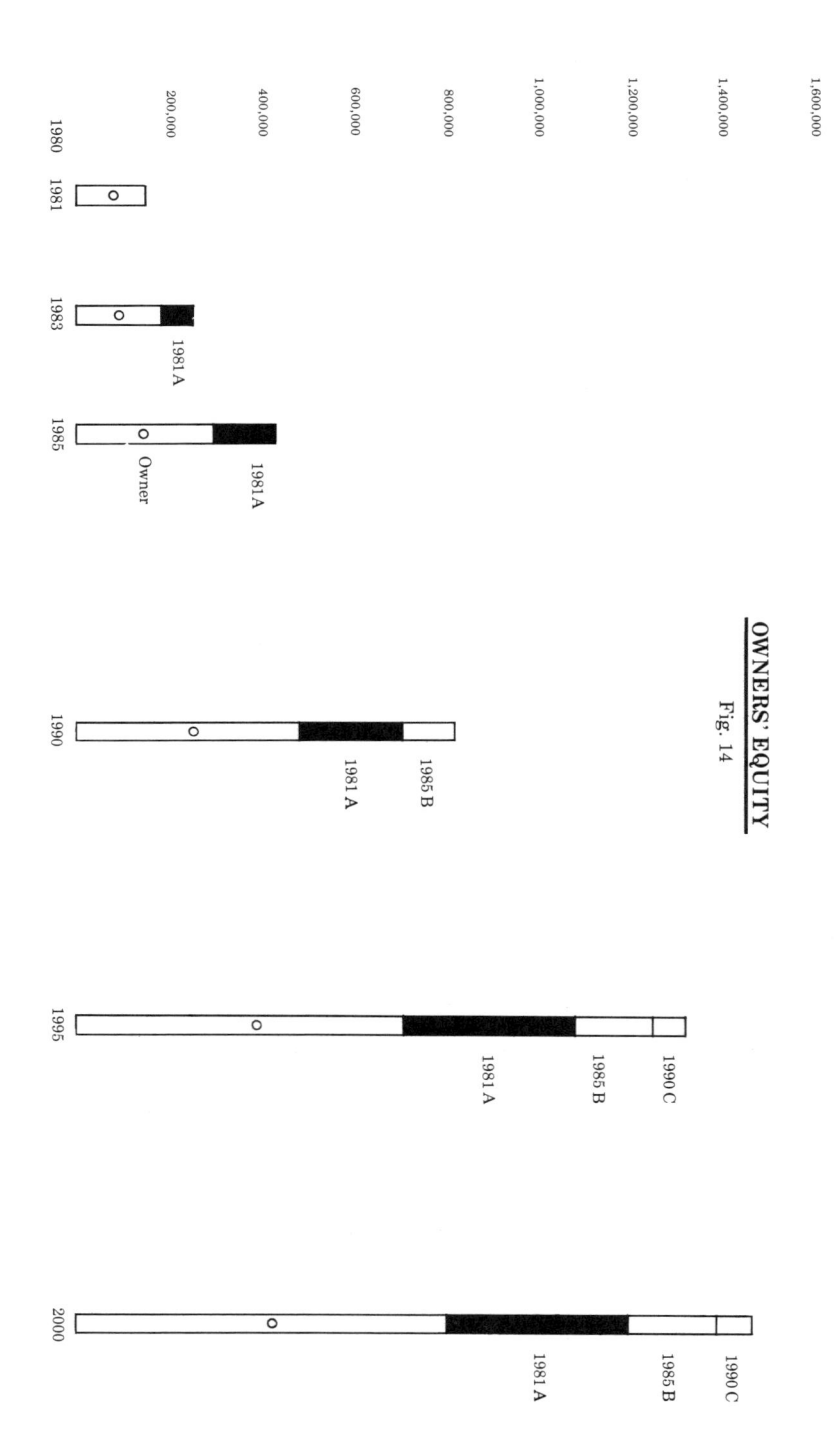

OWNERS' EQUITY
Fig. 14

80

APPENDIX

PRODUCER COMPENSATION SURVEY

The single, most important ingredient that served as a basis of the producer compensation study of the Young Agents Committee of the Independent Insurance Agents of Georgia was a survey that involved 134 participants in the agency ranks.

Each of the participants was asked to rank, by level of importance, nineteen given types of compensation and fringe benefits. The principal purpose of the survey was to test the importance of various compensation and fringe benefits among owners, employed producers and other agency personnel in order to determine the type of benefits that may have to be offered in order to attract persons to the insurance agency business.

The pages that follow provide the results of that survey in four sections.

Section I concerns respondents who are agency owners with (A) up to three years, (B) four to 10 years, and (C) over 10 years experience in the agency business.

Section II concerns respondents who are employed producers with (A) up to three years, (B) four to 10 years, and (C) over 10 years experience in agency work.

Section III concerns respondents who comprise other agency personnel with (A) up to three years, (B) four to 10 years, and (C) over 10 years experience in agency work.

Section IV is the final tabulation of results among all of the respondents.

Producer Compensation

SECTION I (A)

A. Indicate if you are:

　　1. Owner　　　　　　　　　　　　　　Owner

　　2. Employed Producer　　　　　　_____

　　3. Other　　　　　　　　　　　　　_____

B. Indicate the number of years that you have been in the agency business:

　　1. 0 - 3 years　　　　　　　　　　　　4

　　2. 4 - 10 years　　　　　　　　　_____

　　3. Over 10 years　　　　　　　　_____

C. Indicate how important each of the following items of compensation or fringe benefits are to you:

	Very Important	Only Somewhat Important	Not Important At All	Not Sure
1. Salary Only	1	1	2	
2. Commission only	2	2	0	
3. Combination of salary and commission	1	0	2	
4. Security	4	0	0	
5. Company car	0	3	1	
6. Job satisfaction	4	0	0	
7. Expense account	2	1	1	
8. Public recognition	3	1	0	
9. Bonus	3	1	0	
10. Acceptance from others	4	0	0	

Appendix

	Very Important	Only Somewhat Important	Not Important At All	Not Sure
11. Company paid Life & Health Insurance	1	3	0	
12. Ability to control ones income level	4	0	0	
13. Club membership	1	3	0	
14. Mobility (freedom from office confinement)	3	1	0	
15. Company paid education expenses	2	1	0	
16. Transportable skills (being able to take your skill and move to another location)	2	1	1	
17. Ownership	4	0	0	
18. Being able to realize ones full potential as a person	4	0	0	
19. Company contributions to retirement plans	3	1	0	

20. List other fringe benefits and indicate how important they are to you.

Producer Compensation

SECTION I (B)

A. Indicate if you are:

1. Owner — Owner
2. Employed Producer
3. Other

B. Indicate the number of years that you have been in the agency business:

1. 0 - 3 years
2. 4 - 10 years — 27
3. Over 10 years

C. Indicate how important each of the following items of compensation or fringe benefits are to you:

	Very Important	Only Somewhat Important	Not Important At All	Not Sure
1. Salary Only	8	11	3	1
2. Commission only	8	8	7	0
3. Combination of salary and commission	8	7	6	1
4. Security	20	2	1	0
5. Company car	8	10	6	1
6. Job satisfaction	24	0	0	1
7. Expense account	7	11	6	1
8. Public recognition	7	14	4	0
9. Bonus	16	7	2	0
10. Acceptance from others	11	9	4	1

Appendix

	Very Important	Only Somewhat Important	Not Important At All	Not Sure
11. Company paid Life & Health Insurance	13	9	2	1
12. Ability to control ones income level	19	5	0	1
13. Club membership	2	13	9	1
14. Mobility (freedom from office confinement)	15	10	0	0
15. Company paid education expenses	10	13	2	1
16. Transportable skills (being able to take your skill and move to another location)	2	10	12	1
17. Ownership	21	4	0	0
18. Being able to realize ones full potential as a person	20	3	1	0
19. Company contributions to retirement plans	13	7	5	0

20. List other fringe benefits and indicate how important they are to you.

Producer Compensation

SECTION I (C)

A. Indicate if you are:

    1. Owner   Owner

    2. Employed Producer

    3. Other

B. Indicate the number of years that you have been in the agency business:

    1. 0 - 3 years

    2. 4 - 10 years

    3. Over 10 years   7

C. Indicate how important each of the following items of compensation or fringe benefits are to you:

	Very Important	Only Somewhat Important	Not Important At All	Not Sure
1. Salary Only	3	2	1	0
2. Commission only	1	2	0	1
3. Combination of salary and commission	5	0	1	0
4. Security	5	1	1	0
5. Company car	4	1	2	0
6. Job satisfaction	7	0	0	0
7. Expense account	2	3	2	0
8. Public recognition	1	6	0	0
9. Bonus	3	3	0	0
10. Acceptance from others	3	3	0	0

Appendix

	Very Important	Only Somewhat Important	Not Important At All	Not Sure
11. Company paid Life & Health Insurance	5	1	1	0
12. Ability to control ones income level	7	0	0	0
13. Club membership	0	4	3	0
14. Mobility (freedom from office confinement)	6	1	0	0
15. Company paid education expenses	3	3	1	0
16. Transportable skills (being able to take your skill and move to another location)	3	4	0	0
17. Ownership	6	1	0	0
18. Being able to realize ones full potential as a person	7	0	0	0
19. Company contributions to retirement plans	3	3	1	0

20. List other fringe benefits and indicate how important they are to you.

_____ _____ _____ _____ ___

_____ _____ _____ _____ ___

_____ _____ _____ _____ ___

_____ _____ _____ _____ ___

_____ _____ _____ _____ ___

Producer Compensation

SECTION II (A)

A. Indicate if you are:

1. Owner _____
2. Employed Producer _____Employed Producer_____
3. Other _____

B. Indicate the number of years that you have been in the agency business:

1. 0 - 3 years _____42_____
2. 4 - 10 years _____
3. Over 10 years _____

C. Indicate how important each of the following items of compensation or fringe benefits are to you:

	Very Important	Only Somewhat Important	Not Important At All	Not Sure
1. Salary Only	9	22	6	1
2. Commission only	9	14	12	1
3. Combination of salary and commission	31	8	1	0
4. Security	26	9	2	1
5. Company car	7	20	11	3
6. Job satisfaction	36	4	0	1
7. Expense account	15	20	3	2
8. Public recognition	14	17	8	1
9. Bonus	24	15	2	0
10. Acceptance from others	20	20	0	0

Appendix

	Very Important	Only Somewhat Important	Not Important At All	Not Sure
11. Company paid Life & Health Insurance	23	17	1	0
12. Ability to control ones income level	35	6	1	0
13. Club membership	8	22	11	
14. Mobility (freedom from office confinement)	31	10	0	1
15. Company paid education expenses	26	15	1	0
16. Transportable skills (being able to take your skill and move to another location)	13	21	6	0
17. Ownership	28	13	0	1
18. Being able to realize ones full potential as a person	37	5	0	0
19. Company contributions to retirement plans	25	16	1	0

20. List other fringe benefits and indicate how important they are to you.

Producer Compensation

SECTION II (B)

A. Indicate if you are:

    1. Owner   _____

    2. Employed Producer   _____Employed Producer_____

    3. Other   _____

B. Indicate the number of years that you have been in the agency business:

    1. 0 - 3 years   _____

    2. 4 - 10 years   _____27_____

    3. Over 10 years   _____

C. Indicate how important each of the following items of compensation or fringe benefits are to you:

	Very Important	Only Somewhat Important	Not Important At All	Not Sure
1. Salary Only	6	9	5	0
2. Commission only	6	7	8	0
3. Combination of salary and commission	18	3	3	1
4. Security	23	3	0	0
5. Company car	17	7	3	0
6. Job satisfaction	25	2	0	0
7. Expense account	9	13	2	0
8. Public recognition	11	7	7	0
9. Bonus	16	8	1	1
10. Acceptance from others	13	10	3	0

Appendix

	Very Important	Only Somewhat Important	Not Important At All	Not Sure
11. Company paid Life & Health Insurance	22	4	1	0
12. Ability to control ones income level	24	3	0	0
13. Club membership	3	14	9	0
14. Mobility (freedom from office confinement)	18	8	0	0
15. Company paid education expenses	18	8	1	0
16. Transportable skills (being able to take your skill and move to another location)	13	6	6	0
17. Ownership	15	11	1	0
18. Being able to realize ones full potential as a person	25	2	0	0
19. Company contributions to retirement plans	20	6	0	1

20. List other fringe benefits and indicate how important they are to you.

Producer Compensation

SECTION II (C)

A. Indicate if you are:

1. Owner _____

2. Employed Producer _____Employed Producer_____

3. Other _____

B. Indicate the number of years that you have been in the agency business:

1. 0 - 3 years _____

2. 4 - 10 years _____

3. Over 10 years _____3_____

C. Indicate how important each of the following items of compensation or fringe benefits are to you:

	Very Important	Only Somewhat Important	Not Important At All	Not Sure
1. Salary Only	1	1	0	
2. Commission only	1	1	1	
3. Combination of salary and commission	1	1	0	
4. Security	3	0	0	
5. Company car	2	0	1	
6. Job satisfaction	3	0	0	
7. Expense account	2	0	0	
8. Public recognition	1	1	1	
9. Bonus	3	0	0	
10. Acceptance from others	2	1	0	

Appendix

	Very Important	Only Somewhat Important	Not Important At All	Not Sure
11. Company paid Life & Health Insurance	2	1	0	
12. Ability to control ones income level	3	0	0	
13. Club membership	1	1	0	
14. Mobility (freedom from office confinement)	2	0	0	
15. Company paid education expenses	2	0	0	
16. Transportable skills (being able to take your skill and move to another location)	2	0	0	
17. Ownership	1	1	0	
18. Being able to realize ones full potential as a person	2	0	0	
19. Company contributions to retirement plans	1	1	0	

20. List other fringe benefits and indicate how important they are to you.

Producer Compensation

SECTION III (A)

A. Indicate if you are:

  1. Owner _____
  2. Employed Producer _____
  3. Other _____ Other _____

B. Indicate the number of years that you have been in the agency business:

  1. 0 - 3 years _____ 12 _____
  2. 4 - 10 years _____
  3. Over 10 years _____

C. Indicate how important each of the following items of compensation or fringe benefits are to you:

	Very Important	Only Somewhat Important	Not Important At All	Not Sure
1. Salary Only	5	6	0	1
2. Commission only	2	4	4	1
3. Combination of salary and commission	7	2	2	0
4. Security	9	3	0	0
5. Company car	3	4	5	0
6. Job satisfaction	12	0	0	0
7. Expense account	3	7	2	0
8. Public recognition	3	7	2	1
9. Bonus	6	5	1	0
10. Acceptance from others	10	1	0	1

Appendix

	Very Important	Only Somewhat Important	Not Important At All	Not Sure
11. Company paid Life & Health Insurance	7	3	2	0
12. Ability to control ones income level	9	2	1	0
13. Club membership	6	3	2	1
14. Mobility (freedom from office confinement)	5	7	0	0
15. Company paid education expenses	9	2	1	0
16. Transportable skills (being able to take your skill and move to another location)	6	5	1	0
17. Ownership	6	5	1	0
18. Being able to realize ones full potential as a person	11	1	0	0
19. Company contributions to retirement plans	5	6	1	0

20. List other fringe benefits and indicate how important they are to you.

Producer Compensation

SECTION III (B)

A. Indicate if you are:

1. Owner _____
2. Employed Producer _____
3. Other _____ Other _____

B. Indicate the number of years that you have been in the agency business:

1. 0 - 3 years _____
2. 4 - 10 years _____ 10 _____
3. Over 10 years _____

C. Indicate how important each of the following items of compensation or fringe benefits are to you:

	Very Important	Only Somewhat Important	Not Important At All	Not Sure
1. Salary Only	5	4	0	0
2. Commission only	0	2	8	0
3. Combination of salary and commission	3	1	5	1
4. Security	10	0	0	0
5. Company car	3	2	3	2
6. Job satisfaction	10	0	0	0
7. Expense account	1	5	4	0
8. Public recognition	1	7	2	0
9. Bonus	5	4	1	0
10. Acceptance from others	4	5	1	0

Appendix

	Very Important	Only Somewhat Important	Not Important At All	Not Sure
11. Company paid Life & Health Insurance	7	3	0	0
12. Ability to control ones income level	5	5	0	0
13. Club membership	1	5	4	0
14. Mobility (freedom from office confinement)	7	3	0	0
15. Company paid education expenses	6	3	1	0
16. Transportable skills (being able to take your skill and move to another location)	5	2	1	2
17. Ownership	2	3	4	1
18. Being able to realize ones full potential as a person	9	1	0	0
19. Company contributions to retirement plans	8	2	0	0

20. List other fringe benefits and indicate how important they are to you.

_____   _____   _____   _____   _____
_____   _____   _____   _____   _____
_____   _____   _____   _____   _____
_____   _____   _____   _____   _____
_____   _____   _____   _____   _____

Producer Compensation

SECTION III (C)

A. Indicate if you are:

   1. Owner   _____

   2. Employed Producer _____

   3. Other   _____ Other _____

B. Indicate the number of years that you have been in the agency business:

   1. 0 - 3 years   _____

   2. 4 - 10 years   _____

   3. Over 10 years   _____ 2 _____

C. Indicate how important each of the following items of compensation or fringe benefits are to you:

	Very Important	Only Somewhat Important	Not Important At All	Not Sure
1. Salary Only	2	0	0	0
2. Commission only	0	0	1	1
3. Combination of salary and commission	0	0	1	1
4. Security	2	0	0	0
5. Company car	0	1	0	1
6. Job satisfaction	2	0	0	0
7. Expense account	1	0	0	1
8. Public recognition	1	0	1	0
9. Bonus	0	2	0	0
10. Acceptance from others	1	0	1	0

Appendix

	Very Important	Only Somewhat Important	Not Important At All	Not Sure
11. Company paid Life & Health Insurance	2	0	0	0
12. Ability to control ones income level	2	0	0	0
13. Club membership	1	1	0	0
14. Mobility (freedom from office confinement)	2	0	0	0
15. Company paid education expenses	1	1	0	0
16. Transportable skills (being able to take your skill and move to another location)	2	0	0	0
17. Ownership	0	1	1	0
18. Being able to realize ones full potential as a person	2	0	0	0
19. Company contributions to retirement plans	2	0	0	0

20. List other fringe benefits and indicate how important they are to you.

Producer Compensation

SECTION IV

Number of Agents

1. Job Satisfaction 123
2. Being able to realize one's full potential as a person. 117
3. Ability to control one's income level 107
4. Security. 102
5. Mobility (freedom from office confinement). 95
6. Company contributions to retirement plans 84
7. Ownership 83
8. Company paid life & health insurance 82
9. Company paid educational expense 77
10. Bonus. 76
11. Acceptance from others 68
12. Company car 44
13. Expense account 42
14. Public recognition. 42
15. Salary only 40
16. Transportable skills (being able to take your skill and move to another location). 38
17. Combination of salary and commission 36
18. Commission only. 28
19. Club membership 23

INDEX

A

ABC Insurance Agency, 71-80
Accidental death and dismemberment policy, *see* Life Insurance
Accident and sickness insurance, *see* Group Insurance
Achievement, 29
Acquisition of product knowledge, 8
Active partners, 36
Actual estate values, 40
A divided responsibility, 67
Administrative management, 61
Admission to athletic events, 20
Affiliation, 29
Agency business, 2-3, 31-32
Agency career, 3
Agency environment, 49
Agency goals, *see* Job Description and Goal Setting
Agency growth and profits, 38
Agency growth or underwriting profits, 68, 70
Agency hiring, *see* Job Description and Goal Setting
Agency marketing management, 61
Agency ownership, 2-3
    ownership as motivation, 37-40
    transferring ownership, 40-41
Agency perpetuation, 8-9, 57
Agency personnel, 31
Agency placer, 61
Agency premium, 72-78
Agency principals, 5, 62

Agency's balance sheet, 62
Agency's decision-making process and direction, 13
Agency's geographic location, 2
Agency's objective, 5
Agency's operation, 4
Agency's overall operations, 11
Agency's production, 4, 68
Agency's role in training, 11
Agency's training, 4
Agent/Producer Relationship
    application selection, 5
    introduction, 1
    planning for new producer, 1-2
    prospecting for new producer, 3-5
    reasons for entering agency business, 2-3
All-encompassing plan, 45
American Agency System, 62-63
Applicant, *see* Agent/Producer Relationship
Application of principals, goals and objectives, *see* Developing A Producer Compensation Plan
Arts festival, 20
Aspen, Colorado, 20
Association training programs, 11
Atlanta, 20
Authority of new producer, 9
Automobile expense, 18-19
Auxiliary staff functions, 61-70
    benefits, 64-65
    methods of remuneration, 67-70
    responsibilities, 65-67

B

Banking, finance and sales industries, 3
Benefits, 64-65
Bonus arrangement, 16, 29
Bonuses, 44-46, 49-52, 55-56, 58, 62, 68-69
Book of business, 17
Books and manuals, 27
Both personal and commercial lines, 2
Budget
business and personal, 18-19
Business contacts, 4
Business entertainment expense, 19. *See also* Expense Accounts
Buy-sell agreement, 38

C

Cadillac, 19
Car allowances, 46
Career mobility and market ability, 3
Career stimulation motivation, 63
Cash flow problems, 38
Catastrophic medical expenses, 18. *See also* Group Insurance
Central authority, 37
Centralized control, 38
Charitable groups, 28
Charter and state laws, 36
CIC, 13, 21, 57
Civic achievements, 23
Civic club dues, 20
Civic groups, 28
Claims management, 61
Classes of ownership, 35
Client business lunches, 20
Club membership, 28
CLU, 13, 57
College graduate, 3

Combination commission and salary plan, 52
Combination salary-bonus arrangement, 16
Commercial lines, 2
department, 62, 65-67
manager, 65-70
Commission, 44-47, 49-52, 55-56, 58
Commission draw plan, 51
Commission only plan, 50
Common stock, 36
Company automobile, *see* Automobile Expense
Company-owned resort, 28
Compensating producers, *see* Elements of Producer Compensation
Compensation, 2
Compensation arrangements, 43
Compensation package, 17, 46
Compensation plan, 46
Compensation program, *see* Elements of Producer Compensation
Compensation to others, 72-77
Comprehensive plan, *see* Group insurance
Concerts, 20
Consumer of insurance products, 12
Convertible bonds, 37
Corporate decisions, 63
Corporation, *see* Agency Ownership
Cost in training, 4
Country club dues, 20
Country club membership, 11
CPCU, 13, 21, 57

D

Deceased partner, 36

Index

Dental plans, *see* Group Insurance
Developing a producer
   compensation plan, 43-59
      conclusion, 59
      intermediate range goals, 54-56
      long range goals, 56-58
      short range goals, 47-54
Direct income, 49, 55
Direction and ownership of the
   agency, 13, 37
Direct sales expense, 46-47
Disability income, 18. *See also*
   Life Insurance
Double indemnity provisions, *see*
   Life Insurance

E

Education activities, *see*
   Education An Association
   Expense
Education an association
   expense, 21
Education degrees, 29
Educational plan on schedule, 11
Educational responsibilities, 8
Educational studies and
   programs, 13
Effort of formal commercial lines
   department, 66-67
Elements of producer
   compensation, 15-23
     automobile expense, 18-19
     education an associate
       expense, 21
     employee stock option plans, 22
     expense accounts, 19-20
     group insurance, 17-18
     intangibles, 22-23
     life insurance, 18
     retirement plans, 21
     traditional elements, 15
     vacations, 20-21

Employed producers, 31
Employee education and
   training, 3
Employee stock option plans, 22
Employee stock ownership plans
   (ESOP), 40, 45
Employee stock ownership trusts
   (ESOT), 40
Employer funded life insurance,
   18
Entertainment, 46
   expense, 19-20
ESOP, *see* Employee Stock
   Ownership Plans
ESOT, *see* Employee Stock
   Ownership Trusts
Estate planning, 37
Estate problems, 38
Esteem, 29-31
Existing accounts, 9
Exotic cars, 11
Expense accounts, 19-20, 29
Expenses for education, 68-69
Expensive clothes, 11
Experienced person, 4
Extreme rewards, 28. *See also*
   Security

F

Family agencies, 41
Financial gain, *see* Security
Financial interests, 40
Financial obligations, 4
   of producers, 15
Financial status, 31
Food, shelter and clothing, 11
Fringe benefits, 44-45, 49-52,
   55-56, 58. *See also* Job
   Satisfaction
Function of new producer
   both personal and commercial
   lines, 2

commercial lines, 2
inside person or placer of business, 2
personal lines, 2
sales person only, 2

G

Gifts and sales, 40
Goal setting, 1. *See also* Job Description and Goal Setting
Golf tournaments, 20
Good leadership and guidance, 12
Grass roots training, 3
Group health plans, 47
Group insurance, 17-18
Growth of in-house accounts, 38

H

Health and accident insurance, 28
Heirs, 36
Herzberg, Frederick, 28
Hiring and developing new producer, 2
Hiring, *see* Agent/Producer Relationship and Job Description and Goal Setting
Holding companies, 41
Hospital expense plan, *see* Group insurance

I

IIA, 21. *See also* Independent Insurance Agents of America
Inactive partners, 36
Independent agency system, 14
Independent Insurance Agents of America (IIA), 21
Indirect sales expense, 46-47
Inside person or placer of business, 2

Insolvency, 18
Insurance agency business, 32
Insurance experience, 4
Insurance industry associations, 13
Intangibles, 22-23, 32
Inter-agency conflicts, 39
Intermediate goals, 12-13
Intermediate range goals, 8-10, 48, 54-56
Intermediate stage compensation plan, 56
Internal Revenue Service (IRS), 18-19
Intrinsic rewards, 28. *See also* Security
Introduction, *see* Agent/Producer Relationship
IRS, *see* Internal Revenue Service

J

Job description and goal setting
intermediate goals, 12-13
long term goals, 13-14
responsibility and authority, 8-10
short term goals, 10-11
Job satisfaction, 28-29

K

Keough plan, 22
Key underwriters, 63

L

Legal perpetuation, 36
Life insurance, 18, 68-69
Limited ownership, 22. *See also* Intangibles
Liquidating trustee, 35
Liquidation, 37
Long range compensation plan, 58

Index

Long range goals, 8-10, 13-14, 48, 56-58
Long-term financial growth, 5
Loss of motivation, 63

M

Making the proper selection, 5
Management, 9
Markets for accounts, 63
Maslow, Abraham, 27, 29, 31, 37
McClelland's achievement theory, 29
Medical and life insurance, 68-70
Mercedes, 19
Merger or acquisition, 63
Methods of remuneration, 67-70. *See also* Auxiliary Staff Functions
Metropolitan areas, 2. *See also* Automobile Expense
Minority owner, 38-39
Monitoring producer progress, 14
Motivational factors
  esteem, 29
    job satisfaction, 28-29
    security, 27-28
    self needs, 31
    survival, 26-27

N

Need hierachy, 30
New accounts, 8
New producer, 1-2
No formal commercial lines department, 65-66
Noncompete clause, 69-70
Noninsurance industry, 4
Nonsales related expenses, 47
Non-qualified income continuation at retirement plan, 22

O

Occupational level of producer, 28
Office and general expense, 72-77
Office procedures, 26
Office salaries, 47. *See also* Salary
Operas, 20
Operation law, 35
Original owner, *see* ABC Insurance Agency
Owners, 31-32
Owner's equity, 77, 80
Ownership, 5, 35, 44-45, 49-52, 56-58, 68, 72-77
Ownership as motivation, 37-40
Ownership of expirations, 37
Ownership of production, 37, 41

P

Partnership, 35
Performance review, 14
Personal and commercial lines department, 62. *See also* Commercial Lines
Personal interview, *see* Making the Proper Selection
Personal lines, 2
  manager, 65, 68
Personalities of producers, 15
Planning for the new producer, 1-2
Power, 29
Practical perpetuation, 36
Preferred stock, 36-37, 40
Premium income, 71
Private annuity, 40
Producer, *see* ABC Insurance Agency
Producer
  compensating, 2, 15-23

direct and indirect sales expenses, 46
hiring and developing, 2
job description and goal setting, 7-14
monitoring progesss, 14
performance, 13-14
progress, 10
prospecting for, 3-5
responsibilities and goals, 7-14
security and motivation, 46
Producer-agency business relationship, 2
Producer compensation plan, 43-59
Producer compensation programs
all-encompassing plan, 45
sink-or-swim plan, 44
Producer expense
direct sales expense, 46
indirect sales expense, 46
Producer/principal relationship, 43, 46, 48, 54
Producer's family, *see* Job satisfaction
Product/coverage knowledge, 11, 21, 64
Production responsibilities, 8
Professional Insurance Agents, 21
Profit sharing, 29
Property/casualty and other income, 72-77
Prospecting, 9
for new producer, 3-5
Public recognition, *see* Intangibles
Public transporation system, *see* Automobile Expense
Publicly-held agencies, 41

R

Reasons for entering the agency business, 2-3

Relationship of motivation to producer compensation
motivational factors, 26-27
survey results, 31-32
Relationships with others, 9
Religious groups, 28
Rent, 47
Responsibilities
a divided responsibility, 67
effect of formal commercial lines department, 65-66
no formal commercial lines department, 65-66
of job, 3, 8
Responsibility and authority, 8-10
Retirements plans, 21-22, 47, 69-70

S

Salary, 44-46, 49-52, 55-56, 58, 62
Salary arrangement, 15-18. *See also* Elements of Producer Compensation and Survival
Salary-bonus-no contract, 68
Salary-contract-no bonus or ownership, 69
Salary-contract with profit sharing bonus and equity arrangement, 70
Salary-nonrelated bonus-no contract, 68
Salary only plan, 51
Salary-production bonus-contract, 69
Sales ability, 16
Sales expenses, 47, 72-77
Salesperson, 2, 16
San Francisco, 20
Savings account, 17
Security, 27-28
Self needs, 31
Selling skills, 8

Index

Selling techniques, 11
Seminars, 27
Semi-retired life style, *see* Retirement Plans
Service management, 61
Servicing, 9
Short range goals, 8-10, 47-54. *See also* Job Description and Goal Setting
Short term goals, 10-11. *See also* Job Description and Goal Setting
Sickness, disability or death, 57
Single ownership, 37
Sink-or-swim plan, 44
Sole proprietorship 35, 71
Soliciting, 9
Specialized class of business, 2
Stockholder, 71-77
Stock ownership, 73, 75
　　options, 40
　　redemptions, 40
Structure of organization, 28
Survey results, 31-32
Survival, 26-27
Surviving partners, 35-36
Surviving stockholders, 36

T

Taxes, 47
Taylor, Frederick, 25
Time line of an insurance agency, 71-80
Total compensation to owners, 77-79
Training new producer, 11
Transfer ownership, 40-41
Type of business, 2

U

Understanding of agency operations, 8
Underwriting agency manager, 63-64
Underwriting and placing business, 64
Underwriting guidelines, 65
Underwriting management, 61-62
Unskilled person, 4
Utilities, 47

V

Vacations, 20-21, 29
Validation schedules, 52-53
Vested interest, 39
Vesting schedule, 39
Volume of business, 2

W

Work schedule, *see* Job Satisfaction
Written contracts, 39
Written goals, *see* Job Description and Goal Setting
Written job description, *see* Job Description and Goal Setting

Y

Young Agents Committee of the IIA of Ga., 31
Young Agents of Georgia, 17